BAD BEHAVIOUR

REBECCA STARFORD

This edition published in 2023
First published in 2015

This project has been assisted by the Australian Government through the Australia Council for the Arts, its arts funding and advisory body

Allen & Unwin
Cammeraygal Country
83 Alexander Street
Crows Nest NSW 2065
Australia
Phone: (61 2) 8425 0100
Email: info@allenandunwin.com
Web: www.allenandunwin.com

Allen & Unwin acknowledges the Traditional Owners of the Country on which we live and work. We pay our respects to all Aboriginal and Torres Strait Islander Elders, past and present.

A catalogue record for this book is available from the National Library of Australia

ISBN 978 1 76147 015 8

Internal design by Sandy Cull
Set in Berkeley Oldstyle by Midland Typesetters, Australia
Printed and bound in Australia by the Opus Group

10 9 8 7 6 5 4 3 2 1

The paper in this book is FSC® certified. FSC® promotes environmentally responsible, socially beneficial and economically viable management of the world's forests.

Praise for *Bad Behaviour*

'An unflinching examination of the ambivalence, brutality and reckless need for acknowledgement that lies at the heart of so many social cliques and female relationships. Rebecca Starford's memoir of her teenage years at an isolated boarding campus in the Australian bush—and the insidious effect her experiences there had upon the formation of her adult self—is absolutely riveting. At once self-critical, intelligent and beautifully written, *Bad Behaviour* is unforgettable.'
— Hannah Kent, bestselling author of *Burial Rites*

'*Bad Behaviour* is a compelling coming of age story told with honesty and warmth. I was moved by Starford's resilience and insight, simultaneously capturing both the power and powerlessness of being fourteen.'
— Alice Pung, bestselling author of *Unpolished Gem* and *Laurinda*

'*Bad Behaviour* is remarkable. Part *Mean Girls*, part *Lord of the Flies*, yet set in the uncannily familiar Australian terrain of class privilege and bush brutality. With savage urgency, Starford catapults us back to a time of youthful awakening and confusion. Like bystanders at a train wreck, we wonder how the rails could have become so warped and why nobody thought to apply the brakes sooner.'
— Clare Wright, author of *The Forgotten Rebels of Eureka*, winner of the 2014 Stella Prize

'*Bad Behaviour* is not just a beautiful and powerful memoir of a year spent in an Australian boarding school, it is a deftly written psychological study of horrific bullying and all the fear, self-loathing, insecurity, isolation and, yes, courage and desperate camaraderie that often accompanies it. A cautionary tale for parents who love their children so much that they would send them away.'
— David Leser, acclaimed author of *To Begin to Know*

'A raw and disquieting coming of age story, vividly told.'
— Jane Gleeson-White, award-winning author of *Double Entry* and *Six Capitals*

'Rebecca Starford doesn't just nail the toxicity of high school, but captures a viciousness in teenagers so breathtaking, it's almost worthy of Attenborough. Every page of this book adds to a sense of dread that tightens around the reader's neck like a knot. Mandatory reading for every teenage girl.'
—Benjamin Law

'As addictive as Knausgaard. Which is a big call—but I'm making it!'
—Martin Shaw, Readings Bookstore

'An eloquent reminder that love is a place of great vulnerability . . . This is an engrossing book . . . The structure of the book creates a tender bond between a girl and the older version of herself who wants to find her and love her. The warmth of Starford's writing searches honestly for new shapes for her life. It turns stone into clay.'
—Michael McGirr, *Saturday Age*

'A vivid journey into the dark corner where a fourteen-year-old loses her girlhood and has to start becoming a woman. It is also a courageous, fiercely honest assessment of the guilt that we carry from our actions as teenagers; a reckoning of how that guilt accrues through our later lives. If you thought *Lord of the Flies* could only happen among boys, read this book.'
—Malcolm Knox, author of *Wonder Lover*

'Thank goodness that in her year at Silver Creek young Rebecca discovered the solitary consolations of journalling, for this has enabled her astute and frightening rendering of female adolescence. The psychopathic Portia is unforgettable.'
—*The Saturday Paper*, Melbourne

'A confident, engaging, yet frightening look at the teen bullying that has understandably haunted Starford into adulthood.'
—*Weekly Times*, Melbourne

These are my memories.
To protect the privacy of others,
names have been changed,
attributes adjusted, characters conflated
and some incidents condensed.

FOR ELINOR

PROLOGUE

~

It's late, just before lights-out, and we're all tucked up in bed. My book is facedown in my lap, untouched. It's too cold to read; it is the dead of winter, my breath hangs like mist in front of my face. A few beds down, Ronnie is sniping across the aisle at Kendall—'Hey, KFC. Albino pubes. Have you wet yourself tonight?'—and Portia, in the bed beside her, laughs.

All of a sudden Kendall throws back the doona and leaps out of bed, her feet slapping against the floorboards as she makes her way to the light switch. Next minute the dorm goes black and everyone shouts—fifteen voices in a peeved chorus.

Slivers of moonlight shine against the dusty windows. I can just make out Kendall rustling at her bedside table, then she is brandishing something—a can of Impulse. She stands at the top of the aisle, facing out over the beds, and begins to spray up and down her pyjama pants. The sickly scent of musk drifts through the dorm. I hear the lighter click like the sharpening of a switch-blade and a flame shudders in the gloom.

'Watch this,' Kendall murmurs.

And I stare, transfixed, as she moves the lighter down towards her ankle, to the cuff of her pants. It catches the aerosol fumes, and with a great whoosh she is alight, enormous blue flames pulsing up her legs, her face caught in an obscene grimace, her arms thrown wildly in the air.

PART ONE

1

~

When I tell Liv I want to write about Silver Creek, she peers at me over her mug. We're sitting at the breakfast table, still in our pyjamas, the weekend papers strewn about. 'Won't it be strange?' she says, wandering into the kitchen to fix herself a bagel. 'Writing about people you still know?'

Liv went to Silver Creek too, but she had been in a different house with a very different experience. Now, more than ten years later, we live together with another girl, Alice, in a brown-brick terrace in Fitzroy.

I shrug. 'I don't think so. I'm only in touch with one or two Red House girls now, anyway.'

When Liv comes back she looks thoughtful, a deep line etched in her brow. 'It's funny,' she says, biting down on her bagel. 'I can't remember much about Red House, but I do have the clearest memory of visiting. It was really hot—near the start of the year, I think—and some of you were out the front, on the deck. And Portia, she was wandering up and down the steps. Or more like prowling.' She pauses. 'It was like she was the lioness and you were her cubs.'

I put down my coffee. 'Where was I?'

Liv chews, her eyes narrow. 'You know what?' she says. 'I don't remember.'

~

The next morning I leave early, before the rest of the house is up. I drive through empty streets, over a couple of bridges and onto the freeway. After an hour or so, the morning darkens, angry stains against the sky.

Nearer to Silver Creek the landscape changes. The rolling green pastures wash out, as if hardened by the westerly winds. I pass the turn-off to Daisy Road and Cattlemans Flat, and the rock pools. They sound charming. But I know beyond them are other places with other names, like Hell's Kitchen and Razorback Road.

Silver Creek hasn't any signposts. You could drive by, in fact, and never know it was there—the school's seclusion is one of its biggest attractions. So I keep an eye out for the familiar dip, the long sloping paddock and a hay-bale shed at the bottom of the hill. The turn-off torn away like a bite from a cake.

At the cattle grid I pull over and climb out of the car. There are sheep in the front paddock, dozens of them. Their lambs are bounding around, darting one way then another, bleating.

I wander towards the fence. The air smells just as I remember it: sharp, clean, the mildest touch of eucalyptus. And something heavier—earth, perhaps. The wind whips at the stray leaves around my feet.

During one agriculture lesson I was taught how to remove sheep's tails. Docking, the teacher had called it. The class had broken into groups to gather up a few sheep, tethering their legs so they couldn't kick or run away, before a thick elastic band was placed around the top of the tail. But I had stood off in the corner of the paddock, refusing to do it. I hated seeing the sheep writhing like that, their pained eyes.

'It's for their *own good*,' the teacher shouted, throwing his hands up in the air. The rest of the class turned to look at me, surprised; it was, I think, the first time I was disobedient in a lesson.

I glance towards the car. My old Silver Creek diary sits on the back seat on top of a pile of sweaters and scarves. It's an ordinary Collins day-to-a-page, with a picture of Little Miss Naughty pasted on the front cover, along with photographs of my friends.

The night before I'd sat down and read the whole thing through. It was unsettling to rediscover those words from so long ago, somehow invasive—that fourteen-year-old seemed a stranger to me. I had been a diligent diarist, writing entries most days, filling the pages with anecdotes, scraps of letters, recounts of conversations. Where the entries were short I had sticky-taped Cadbury wrappers, newspaper clippings or pictures of Prince William to the bottom of the page.

But what bothered me most were all the gaps in the diary. So many things had been left out entirely—arguments, sadness, misbehaviour. On these pages I'd instead pasted in photographs from hikes, to make it look like something else had happened. What, I wondered, was I trying to forget?

The sky is turning black, like ink spilt across a table. Rain will come—I can smell it.

Climbing back in the car I reach for the diary. On the inside cover is a photograph of the Red House girls. It is night; we are dressed for bed. Fifteen smiling girls. Portia isn't in the photo. She must have taken it.

I trace my finger over each girl. Simone, Lou and Emma, Emma's arm slung around Lou's shoulder. Ronnie and Briohny, side by side in the middle, grinning like they're sharing a joke. And Kendall, at the back, her white hair drawn into a loose plait. She was pretty when she smiled, I realise with shock.

The diary had hardly mentioned Kendall, or what happened to her. But I haven't forgotten—how could I? Some memories are like bore water, cold and dark and deep beneath the ground. That's the real reason I have come back: to understand where it all went wrong. Maybe if I'd known how much the events of that year would come to shape me I would have tried harder to change what happened. I hadn't told Liv about that.

The girls in the photograph seem happy—smiling with their eyes. I look at myself, in the front row, dressed in a green-and-white cotton pyjama top. My hair is out, straggly, very blonde. I look boyish, my face young and round. There are bags under my eyes. I can just see the beginnings of my braces behind my lips. And I'm not smiling, not even with my eyes.

I don't remember posing for Portia, or the night we all stood like that, so relaxed in each other's company—I don't remember any of it. But that girl in the photo is looking at me.

2

~

We stop in Hay, a small town about an hour and a half from Silver Creek, pulling into the car park near a brown dunny block. Mum peers into the rear-view mirror to reapply her lippy. Cinnamon Toast—I catch a perfumey hint of it. She buys it from David Jones in town.

Milling around the bakery door are a few Silver Creek boys. I can tell they're on the way to school from the way they're dressed: boat shoes and polo shirts, faded pairs of school-issue khaki shorts.

Mum and I sit near the drinks fridge. We've ordered coffees and cake, but I'm not at all hungry. I stare at the table as the boys' laughter chimes off the tiled walls.

'Are you all right, darling?' Mum asks.

A bit of froth is smeared above her lip. I glance away, across the bakery. The boys are getting louder now. They're excited, I realise with a sickening feeling. They can't wait to get to Silver Creek and say goodbye to their families. Tears sting in the corner of my eyes. Mum is reaching now, for my sweaty hand, but I sit back.

'I'm fine,' I say, and force myself to smile. I don't want her to worry about me.

~

We drive on, past Ronald Lake and more straw-coloured paddocks. I chew at my fingernails, tearing at the cuticles until specks of blood appear. There are no telephones at Silver Creek, or laptops or internet or television, so I'll have to write letters to stay in touch with Mum and Dad and my brother Archie. For the next year I'll be living in a wooden house with fifteen other girls. The boys live on the other side of the campus. We'll have regular school each day, just like every other fourteen-year-old, but we'll spend the rest of our free time outdoors, running and hiking, building huts and cultivating the vineyard, and in the winter months we will ski and take part in community service.

I learnt all this from the information session last year, where staff and former students spoke to our class and later showed us slides of the bush campus. It had sounded quaint at the time, like something out of Enid Blyton, but now I'm not so sure.

It takes us two passes to find the turn-off, hidden in the grassy slope. The car shudders over the drive. We pass the vineyard, the piggery and the vegetable garden, and an old tractor parked in a paddock of dry grass. The road curves through overgrowth. On the other side the drive extends up the slope, beyond what I recognise as the enormous dining hall and hayshed.

'Gosh, it's like a farm, isn't it?' Mum says.

She parks near the library and asks if I'm coming to find out what house I'm in. I shake my head. She sighs, opening the car door and stalking off across the gravel.

A whole year, I keep telling myself. *I'm going to be away from home for a whole year.* The next time I'll see my family will be at the end of first term, in nearly three months. The longest I've been away from home before is a week on last year's school ski trip.

'You're in Red House,' Mum announces when she returns, smiling now. 'The new house. Simone is in with you too.'

Simone is a friend from the junior campus in the city where I had been a student for the past three years. There were only five girls in our class, so I suppose I'm lucky to have a friend. But panic starts to flutter in my chest. What if Simone and I get into another fight, like we did last year, and everyone gangs up on me again, calling me names like Bugs Bunny because of my bad teeth? I glance at Mum, stricken. She is watching me, frowning. I don't think she can read my face, or perhaps she is afraid to. If I asked her now, would she turn around and drive me home? Would she and Dad get their money back?

'Shall we?' she says, starting the car.

Red House is at the top of the campus. Mum drives on, so slow now it would be faster to walk. I drum my fingertips against the dash, feeling sweat start to prickle on my chest and under my arms.

Where the road curves a group of boys is gathered out the front of a house. They all stop talking and stare as we pass, as if they've never seen a car before. Just as we roll by, the afternoon sun flares against the windscreen and I raise a hand to shield my face, realising a second later, with embarrassment, that it must look like I'm waving to them.

'They're nice-looking boys,' Mum says. 'Aren't they, darling?'

'*Mum.*'

After more bends and another long stretch of road, we finally arrive.

I climb out of the car and gaze up the dusty slope. Red House is a large brown building, about a hundred feet long, with a tin roof. Pieces of timber lie at the bottom of the drive and piles of gravel have been dumped in the ditch near the road.

'Well,' Mum says, eyes flickering over the wood. 'This is something.' The land around the building has been cleared, almost razed.

When I start to pull bags from the boot, Mum puts a hand on my arm. 'Why don't you go up first,' she says. 'Just to say hello to everyone. You don't want me hanging around like a bad smell.'

I glance towards the brown house, my mouth turning chalky. Mum is standing at the boot, and she nods at the path.

'Go on,' she says, passing me a suitcase.

But when I get there the dormitory is empty. I stand in the doorway, gazing around the large, warm room. Sun glows at the windows, motes of drifting dust caught in the light. Grime coats the polished boards and skirting. It smells of paint and wood sanding.

Sixteen narrow beds are spaced evenly around the dorm, each with small wheels and ugly metal railings. Beneath the beds are two drawers and an accompanying side table. Most beds are made up, a school tartan thrown over the mattress, a few posters Blu-tacked to the wall. James Hird is in full flight, the *Cleo* Bachelor of the Year, chiselled and glistening in a black-and-white spread.

I leave my suitcase in the doorway and have a quick look around the rest of the house. Attached to the dorm is the study, with a large fireplace in the centre. Some desks already have books on them, but most are empty.

Nametags are stuck on the desks and I find mine is nearest the door. This is where I'll have to sit for our two hours of prep each night, after dinner and before bed. I know about prep from the well-thumbed prospectus kept on top of the microwave in the kitchen at home: it's what boarding schools call homework.

Next to the study is a small kitchen with a toaster and kettle, and lockers built into the wall to store our snacks sent from home. Not snacks, I remind myself, but *tuck*.

Around the side is the boiler room with piles of old newspapers and a bin full of kindling. In the middle is a blackened cast-iron boiler for the house's hot-water supply. The deck overlooks the drive and a stooping basketball hoop, a small shed shaped like a kennel and filled with wood, and an axe lying beside a block. At the back is an expanse of dense bush, full of gums and wattles and other trees I don't know the names for. I can't see any fences or gates.

Back inside, I drag my suitcase along the floor. There are a few girls in the dorm now, sitting on beds. The beds are also arranged alphabetically and I find mine in the middle, covered in stuff—a doona, clothes, books and a bag. A sullen girl sits on the next bed, chewing gum. She's wearing jeans torn at the knee and a pair of tatty boots. She eyes me up, half smiling, freckles scattered across her nose. Another girl sits beside her and she grins at me quickly before looking away.

'I guess you want me to move that?' says the girl with freckles, nodding towards my bed. Her own area is neat, with a few photographs propped up on the bedside table.

'If you don't mind,' I murmur.

I feel the girls' eyes on me as I unpack. Once or twice I look up to see them watching. The shy girl's name, I discover, is Lou. The other girl is Emma.

'You know everyone else here?' she asks.

I shake my head. 'Not really.'

Finally they rise from their beds, mutter to each other in low voices. I hold my breath, willing them to go. But they linger, staring down at my nametag.

'Rebecca,' says Emma. Slowly, like a challenge. Lou giggles, her head lowered, shrinking into herself. I catch sight of her hands, her long fingers, grubby nails. They are trembling.

~

I've brought too many clothes. Woollen jumpers, polar fleeces, shirts and shorts, as well as work boots, casual shoes and running shoes bulge from my shelves. Socks and underwear make up most of my first drawer—I've a dozen pairs of hiking socks, a week's worth of running socks and another of day socks, and as many pairs of undies and bras. Toiletries, towels, pyjamas, bedding, a couple of blankets, and handkerchiefs stacked like a wad of cash.

I'm adjusting my doona cover when a young woman appears in the dorm. 'You must be Rebecca,' she calls, smiling.

This is Miss Lacey, the head of Red House. How is that possible? I wonder, looking at her more closely. She seems barely an adult herself, bouncing on the balls of her feet, her blonde hair tied high in a scrunchie. She darts around the dorm, and after inspecting my drawers and my tog room locker where my hike gear is stored, she nods in satisfaction.

Next she takes Mum aside to explain some of the house rules, pointing to the jobs roster, which is a pie chart hanging from the wall.

'And where are your living quarters?' Mum asks, glancing around the dorm.

Miss Lacey laughs. 'Oh, I don't live here! My house is down the road. No, the girls are very much on their own. It's deliberate, of course, so the houses can be self-regulating.'

'I see,' says Mum.

Miss Lacey wanders to my bedside, picking up one of my pink-haired trolls. 'I've heard a lot about you, Rebecca,' she says. 'I'm looking forward to big things.'

She is talking about my scholarship. Every teacher seems to know about it long before I meet them. On my first day at the junior campus, the scholarship kids were lined up at assembly for a special introduction. I suppose they thought it nice to single us out, but it only made me feel like an outsider, and since then I've always worried that the teachers would expect much more of me than of everyone else.

But when I look up Miss Lacey just smiles, her eyes crinkling, and I know, instantly, she isn't like other teachers, that I want to be her friend. And I guess I *am* different in this place, which over the years has had princes and future politicians and media heirs and heiresses as students.

'Now,' she says, standing tall. 'You already know Simone, but what about the others?'

There are no clues in quilts or teddy bears. I shake my head.

'No problem.' She checks her watch. 'You can meet the rest of the house at dinner, which is at six o'clock tonight. Try not to be late.'

After Miss Lacey has gone, Mum rifles through her handbag for her car keys. 'I better make a start home,' she says.

I walk her to the deck, staring at her hand, which hangs loose at her side. I want to hold it. Her leaving seems wrong. This should be happening to another girl, someone who lived a hundred years ago, in England. Not to me.

'Make sure you eat properly,' Mum says, slinging her handbag over her shoulder. 'Don't stay up talking too late at night, either. You'll need your sleep.'

She smiles and her teeth shine in the shadows. 'And don't forget to write,' she says.

Mum's eyes seem enormous. I nod, knowing she is anxious about what I might say. Mum's old friends from her university days always remark on how alike we are. That we have the same round face, the same bump in our nose. It used to make me cringe hearing that, but now I feel a painful swell of pride, which is unexpected and confusing, and my eyes drop to the ground.

'Well, bye-bye, darling.' Her lips brush against my cheek. 'See you soon, okay?'

I watch her walk down the gravel path and climb into the driver's seat. She sits there for a moment, unmoving, then in the dim interior light she reapplies her lippy. Seeing me watching she waves. I want to run to the car and throw open the passenger door. I want to go home with her and never come back here. But when the car rolls past, I raise my hand. 'It's okay,' I say under my breath. 'It's okay.'

I stay out on the deck until the sun has sunk behind the hills. Smoke drifts through the air. A small flame robin perches on the banister, tweeting to other birds in low-hanging branches. I watch them until a thick feeling forms in my throat. This isn't how I imagined my arrival—I had pictured the open arms of instant new friends, laughter and smiles. Not this deep, black loneliness.

Ten minutes before six, I set off along the same road we'd driven up only a couple of hours ago. On my way I pass a brown house with a light on in the front room and children's laughter breaks through the quiet. I don't really know where I'm going, only that if I head down the hill I'll eventually find the dining hall.

I veer off the road, down a stone path beside the chapel, which is an enormous A-frame set high above the classrooms. It's spooky walking through the school for the first time like this, on my own, the sound of my footsteps bouncing off the empty buildings. Normally I'd love creeping around in the half-light, inventing all kinds of scenarios that made the school so still and silent (an invasion, maybe, or a deadly plague?). But tonight

I long for noise. Television, the radio bleating talkback, Dad clattering in the kitchen.

Near the art school are some concrete steps leading to another road. Between the trees I glimpse a few boys running, their liquid movement like dogs on a hunt. Finally I reach the top of the stairs overlooking the amphitheatre and the dining hall, whose enormous green roof is camouflaged against the grassy slope. I linger here for a moment, my heart throbbing in my chest. Kids are everywhere, a couple of hundred at least. Two teachers patrol the landing.

I glimpse Simone in the line furthest from the stairs and feel a surge of relief. But when I take my place at the back, no one turns to say hello, not even Simone. All eyes are fixed to the front, on the teachers barking out the roll call. *Where am I going to sit?* My guts are burning at this thought until I become aware that the girl in front has turned around and is gesturing at me. My name was called and I didn't even hear it.

~

Dinner is flame-grilled chicken with soggy vegetables and packet mash. It smells like the food served in hospitals. But this is a good meal, apparently—the dining hall always serves the best meals on the first day of term or when we are about to see our parents.

Seating around the table is crowded. I can barely move to reach for anything. Not that I'm hungry. When I dare to look around, I recognise a few faces from the main campus, which everyone calls the Big School; girls I've met once or twice at the interschool athletics or swimming carnivals. They probably wouldn't remember me—the Big School girls always looked down on us at those gatherings. The rest of the girls around the table appear to be new.

After we'd filed into the dining hall, Simone had motioned for me to sit next to her. She's already struck up a conversation with the girl on her other side. I'm thankful for the chatter—it means I don't need to do much talking. She's telling a story I've heard before and I relax a little, sipping at my cordial.

Emma and Lou sit across the table, deep in their own conversation. Lou is very pretty, pale-skinned with a soft blush on her high cheekbones. There is something sturdier about Emma, brasher, with the gap between her teeth and those obnoxious freckles. But she has a kind smile.

'That's Portia down there,' Simone murmurs, nodding towards the end of the table where girls have their backs turned. I can't really see Portia, just the crop of her dark hair and a thick brown arm, which I glimpse as she reaches for the salt.

'And that's Veronica next to her. But everyone calls her Ronnie. Apparently Portia and Ronnie nearly got expelled last year from the Big School.'

I chew on a stale piece of bread. 'Oh yeah?'

'Yeah. And the deputy headmaster told them they should be tied to the fountain in the quadrangle and flogged.' Simone frowns. 'Is he even *allowed* to say that?'

I have a better view of Ronnie. She has auburn hair and a smooth angular face. When she turns, I see her eyes are a silky green colour—I don't think I've ever seen a girl more beautiful. She could be a *Dolly* model. But there is something else about her demeanour, something nearly savage in the way she shovels food into her mouth and throws her long arms around. I don't know why but it troubles me, and I drag my eyes away.

'Ronnie lives in Brunei,' Simone continues, in a whisper now. 'Her dad does some sort of work in mining.'

'She looks a bit . . . intense,' I say.

'Well, I heard she's been a boarder since she was *six*. I guess that's why she's a bitch.'

At the end of the table Red House's slushie, Kendall, serves the last of the food from a trolley. On a weekly rotation, the slushie—a girl or boy from the particular house—serves everyone's breakfast, lunch and dinner, as well as clearing the dirty crockery and cutlery and taking it through to the stinking industrial washer deep in the belly of the kitchen.

Kendall's movement around the trolley is quiet, careful, and her gaze is lowered the whole time. When she does look up, I see how bright her blue eyes are, with lashes so fair they're almost invisible.

Once I've looked at her properly I find I can't stop. It's her hair; white-blonde and gathered in a plait that hangs to her waist. She's dressed in a T-shirt many sizes too big and no-brand jeans, which is at odds with the Canterbury sweaters and brown T-bars that are the predominant fashion of the dining hall.

'Ken-*daaall*!' Ronnie bangs her glass on the tabletop. 'More cordial. *Please*.'

As Kendall lopes off Ronnie says something that makes the girls around her swivel. They watch Kendall cross the floor before laughing, Ronnie's shriek piercing the hall. As they rock back and forth, wheezing over their chicken, Portia turns and catches my eye.

There is chatter around the dorm before lights-out but I stay quiet, reading my book. A couple of girls sneak into the tuck room where they stay for hours, the thick line of yellow light glowing beneath the door.

It takes me a long time to fall asleep. I can't stop thinking about Mum driving away and how I wish I'd told her I love her.

I wake during the night, my heart pounding. Hunger scrabbles at my stomach. I sit up and look over the dorm. How menacing it seems in the moonlight. Settling back down, I notice Lou beside me, propped up by her pillows, staring into space.

The next morning she is already up and dressed before I wake, hunched over the bed and tinkering with her watch. 'You make noises in your sleep, you know,' she says.

I squirm beneath the doona. 'Sorry. Hope I didn't sound like a freak.'

Her laugh is high-pitched, more like a bird than a person. 'No,' she says. 'You sound like a kitten.'

She looks at me then, still shy, and we both smile.

3

Classes begin the following day and I discover school at Silver Creek isn't much different from last year. There are two periods in the morning, two after recess, and another two in the afternoon. We don't have to wear school uniform, so I dress in an old pair of jeans and Dad's brown jumper. Most kids wear an item of uniform anyway, usually a grey jumper with a blue band, or a long-sleeved sports sweater.

Our form groups are called sets. I'm in Set 4, along with Ronnie, and we share English, Science, Maths, Religion, Art, PE and Outdoor Education. The sets are mixed with kids from all different houses—boys and girls. I don't know any boys in my set. They don't really talk to the girls, sitting instead at the back of the classroom in a long surly line, chairs tilted beneath their desks. Only in the labs do we have to sit in alphabetical order, which means I share a desk with Ronnie and a boy named Rich Browne.

I had expected Ronnie to be wildly extroverted, but she is quiet and rather studious in class, scribbling down notes in handwriting full of circles and stars. In fact she hardly says a word to me, except to ask if she might borrow my eraser from time to time.

But at lunchtime she saves me a seat at the table next to Portia. Huddled together, they talk about their classes. Portia does most of the talking, complaining about the teachers—'Isn't Mr Greig just *foul*? What a toad!'—which makes Ronnie laugh.

Up close, Portia's face is as brown as her arms, and she has freckles scattered across the bridge of her nose. Her eyes are a dull blue, with steely flecks around the small irises, and her face is square and flat. She isn't pretty at all; rather boyish, really. But there is something magnetic about her. I don't want her to stop talking.

'Anyone you don't like in your set, Starford?' she asks, biting down on an apple.

It's strange to be called *Starford*, but it seems everyone at Silver Creek has some sort of nickname, most often based on their surname: Willo, Rusty, Smithy.

I wipe my mouth, giving Ronnie a sideways look. 'Well,' I say, 'the other girls are pretty annoying.'

'Yeah?' Portia says, edging forward. 'Who?'

'*Lauren*,' Ronnie drawls. 'What a sucky bitch. Like in English—her hand was up for *every* question. Wasn't it, Bec?'

'Yeah,' I say, shifting in my seat. 'Total suck.'

At the end of lunch, before Kendall clears our plates away, the cowbell is struck a few times and everyone falls quiet as Mr Bishop, the running master, stands up. He's young, with dark hair turning grey at the temples. He threads his way through the tables, explaining how after school every student is required to line up outside the library for our first *crossie*.

A few girls on our table glance at one another, confused, but I know all about crossies from the prospectus. They're compulsory cross-country runs, held most days of the week. Each term the route will change, growing longer and harder. This first route, Mr Bishop says, is around six kilometres—'A walk in the park,' he drawls.

As well as the crossies, we all have to participate in a weekly 'long run', a ten- to fifteen-kilometre race; there's one scheduled for the next day. This elicits a few mutters from around the hall.

'As most of you know,' Mr Bishop continues, louder now, 'this running is in preparation for the Silver Creek Marathon, a thirty-two-kilometre race in the final week of the school year. The fruits, if you like, of months and months of hard physical work.'

There are more groans now. Mr Bishop laughs and sits back down. 'Rotten fruit, more like,' I hear Emma mutter from the other end of our table.

It is the hottest time of the day. The dry, baking heat shimmies from concrete and makes long grass coil. Boys are dressed in football shorts and navy singlets, girls in bike shorts and crop tops, some with white socks pulled up to the knee.

I move to the front of the line. I'm looking forward to this. I'm a good runner; I was on the athletics squad last year and all summer I did training runs with Dad.

He's always encouraged my running. Before I was born he was a football umpire, so fit he could run for hours at a time. We often head out together for an afternoon run. It's never far: past the hospital and along the footpath next to the train tracks, then past the bowls club and the park where people take their dogs, and down the street with the strip of blue water on the horizon. I always turn off for home at the big house with the attic, glimpsing Dad before he disappears behind a hedge.

One time I went further on, all the way to the beach, and as we jogged along the sand Dad began yelling at anyone with his or her dog off the leash. 'Read the signs,' he shouted. 'On the leash. *On. The. Leash!*' He gestured angrily, his voice growing more manic with each stride, while I ran along beside him, too breathless with embarrassment to sprint away.

I'm still turning over this memory when the teacher blows a whistle. The scrum tightens, and someone jabs me in the ribs. I don't know the etiquette for this crossie—is it a race too? But before I can ask the gun is fired and everyone bolts in a billow of dust. For a moment I'm disorientated and, jostling for space and air, I drop behind the pack, eyes fixed on the clay road.

The pack loosens when the boys make a dash for the front. Most girls run in pairs, their ponytails swishing with each stride. At the bottom of the road are the cattle grid and a stile, which I climb to make my way up Dusty Hill.

I stop at the drink stand at the top, doubled over, drawing in long, ragged breaths. My head is sweating and a stitch pierces my side. I glance at my watch, shocked to see I've only run for ten minutes. More kids fly by.

I gaze across the yellow fields, the sky a solid blue, like a colour from a painting, and I think of Dad again. He'd love all this dust and sweat, this heat. He'd tell me I was lucky to be living in such a beautiful part of the world.

I wobble down the hill towards another large paddock. The path is so dry that once or twice my feet slide out from under me. I lurch across the creek, cool air swelling from the shallows. A few black birds watch me from spindly gums.

The final leg steers me back up the school drive. Hordes of kids line the embankment, clapping and cheering—it looks like most of the school have finished the race. Portia sits on the highest spot, among a group of boys, and she calls out, 'Go, Starford,' as

I stagger across the finish line. A timecard is thrust in my hands and Miss Lacey appears from somewhere to give me a pat on the shoulder. 'Well done,' she says. But I have ranked badly.

Back at the house, girls are everywhere. I don't want to talk to anyone after the disappointment of the race, but there is nowhere to go, so I end up sitting on the toilet. When I come out, Emma asks how I went.

I wipe my brow. 'Yeah,' I say, 'really well.'

That night I write to Dad. I tell him about the crossie and how happy I am with my time. I'm surprised how easily the lies come, spilling like an oil slick. When I read over the letter, I begin to forget what actually happened and another memory starts to form, taking shape like my words on the page.

I wake early the next morning to pain pulsing through my body. My shins are especially tender, and my head is splitting: the first hint of a migraine. I hobble to the tog room for aspirin. Shuffling back I pause in the doorway. The girls are still asleep, hardly stirring. When I return to bed I tug at the covers, glancing back across the dorm. I start in fright. Kendall has sat up, the sheet wrapped around her shoulders, and is watching me.

~

Already I can see attachments forming in the house. Pairs, mostly—Ronnie and Portia, Lou and Simone. The latter sit together at every meal, wait for each other after chapel; sometimes they even brush each other's hair before we go to bed.

I see all this because I am looking for it. In the house, I am still an observer, rather than a participant. I am quiet, hardly talking to anyone unless they talk to me first. This reticence, while not a surprise, worries me. I had hoped to have thrown it off by now.

No one else seems to be sad, or lonely, or missing their family. I don't know if I miss my parents—it's too soon to tell. They haven't written to me yet. Most girls have had letters from home. Some have even received parcels of tuck. But there isn't time to dwell on home. Every day is filled with activities: school, crossies, swims at the dam, jobs around the campus. And soon we start hiking.

More than the crossies or the long runs, the hiking is what I have been most looking forward to. Every weekend in the summer and spring months, we will trek out in the wilderness, without parents or teachers. Chart our own routes, reading the maps stuffed in the pockets of our packs, surviving on our wits and instincts—it's the stuff of adventure novels. They start as overnighters, covering fifteen or twenty kilometres. But they build until, eventually, we all embark on the Final Hike, the pinnacle of the school year. Like the runs, the hikes are compulsory, and it doesn't matter if it's bushfire baking or raining a deluge; they are never cancelled.

The first hike is a day trip up Mount Silver Creek with the rest of Red House. Some girls have never even been camping before, let alone spent a night in the bush. 'Princesses,' Emma laughs, giving me a wink, as she shoves a water bottle into her pack.

I've never walked up a mountain from top to bottom and I'm nervous about being slow, even though Miss Lacey has assured me that Mount Silver Creek is only small, about thirteen hundred metres above sea level. I have, however, done a lot of camping. Most holidays my parents packed up the car with weeks' worth of supplies and headed off to remote places like Wilpena Pound in the Flinders Ranges, Kangaroo Island, or Porepunkah at the foot of Mount Buffalo. We slept in the big family tent on these holidays, and when it was very cold Dad would let me climb into his sleeping bag to get warm.

When Archie and I got older, Mum and Dad traded in the tent for a campervan, with a built-in sink and an oven, and double beds sprouting at each canvased end. In the evening we'd play board games or listen to the quiz on the ABC. I remember the sounds of these nights so clearly: the rustle of nighttime creatures in trees, the low drone of insects, the faint lap of the river against its banks. And even though I was sharing that tiny space with my family for weeks and weeks, I still managed to find time on my own. If I didn't want to talk, no one made me.

Now I would be spending nights in the bush with a large group of fourteen-year-old girls—a prospect that thrills and terrifies me in equal measure. What if I don't feel like talking when we make dinner? What if they want to tell jokes around the campfire and I can't think of any? Or, worse, what if they want to *sing*? I wonder if I can bring a book with me. I doubt it.

~

As Miss Lacey leads us on our first hike, she explains how back in the olden days the hiking had been so competitive that boys sometimes walked through the night: trekking to Blairgowrie Hut and on to the main range from Mount Howard to Mount Farrier, then back around to The Overpass and The Promontory. Some went even further south to Trent Hut, covering hundreds of kilometres.

After we stop for a drink, Portia and Ronnie move to the front, flanking Miss Lacey, their legs moving like watery shadows beneath their packs. Other girls, like Kendall, lag further behind. Everyone is paired up, but I walk by myself.

Eventually I get stuck in the middle of the group behind Briohny. She's the kind of girl I imagine from the 1950s, with a clean and creamy complexion, and a soft yet sturdy build. She's pretty, I suppose, but her face always seems trapped in a scowl, nose crinkled like she's caught a bad smell. Ronnie has already given Briohny the nickname *Whiony*, and she does whine about almost everything—the running, the heat, schoolwork, dining hall food, the lumps in her mattress. She whines about all the teachers, other girls, the boys too—'Why can't I get a boyfriend?' she'll sigh, and no one knows where to look.

We stop under some trees so the slow girls can catch up. When they do, Briohny points at Kendall. 'You're holding us up on purpose.'

A titter moves through the group.

'We're all going at our own pace, Briohny,' Miss Lacey says, stepping forward. 'It's important to be patient.'

Briohny scoffs, throwing Kendall another dirty look. She turns to me. 'Can you smell that?' she says, quiet so no one else will hear.

'What?'

'Piss,' Briohny sneers. 'She pisses herself. So bad she has to wear nappies.'

'*What?*'

'Look at her arse.' She nods towards Kendall, who at this moment is bending over to retrieve her pack. 'Can't you see it?'

Kendall is struggling. Her cheeks are blotched scarlet and she's sweating profusely. Every now and then she tugs at her white shorts, which are bunched up around her bottom. It could be from a pad. But when my eyes drop to her legs I see they've gone blue, like the plucked chickens hanging from hooks at the market—a thought that immediately fills me with shame.

When the group moves off I make a push to the front, where Portia is now telling a story about a party where she got so drunk she vomited in a shoe. I want to hear about the party—I've never been drunk before—but I soon tire of walking so fast, and fall behind again.

I stop, my chest tight, and adjust my straps. My pack is so heavy it feels like I'm dragging another person along. Emma draws up beside me. 'You okay?' she asks.

An hour later we reach the top. I throw off my pack, the cool breeze at my back. I feel queasy, and lean against a tree to catch my breath.

A few girls wander off to take photographs, while others sit around a cluster of rocks, snacking on sandwiches and drinking orange Tang. Miss Lacey doesn't seem tired at all. 'It sounds crazy now,' she says, smiling, 'but at the end of the term you'll all be running up Mount Silver Creek.'

I turn to Emma and roll my eyes.

'Fuck that,' she groans.

~

Back at school, everyone showers and gets dressed for formal dinner. Blue-and-white-striped dresses, grey jumpers, black shoes with long white socks. After a day of hiking, my uniform feels crisp, like cardboard.

After dinner we have a Eucharist service. The chapel is my favourite building at Silver Creek. Inside it's plain, unembellished—there's an altar at the front, of course, which is bare except for a large gold crucifix resting on the Communion table. Behind the cross the enormous windows overlook the trees, a technicolour of blue and green and yellow. I like chapel more than I expected. My parents aren't at all religious—I'm not baptised—and I can't think of a time my family have been in a church together. Religion and God have always been stuffy things to me, as if shrouded in a mouldy velvet curtain. But here I enjoy the readings from the Scripture. The best part of the morning service is the time at the end for quiet reflection. At first I found it difficult to sit on the cold pews and think about nothing. Now

I look forward to it; I close my eyes and listen to the shuffle of shoes on the bluestone floor.

This evening the chaplain, Father Wilson, gives a sermon on Silver Creek. He talks about the origins of the school, and the founder, an Englishman who in the 1950s bought the land at great expense to establish the campus—a risky prospect so soon after the war. It had been a boys' school at first. Girls only came here twenty years ago.

'While a great many things have changed since Professor Duncan founded Silver Creek,' Father Wilson says, his voice echoing around the cloisters, 'the values of our school have remained unchanged. You are still removed from the comfortable and familiar—your televisions, your computers, your friends and family. For some, this feels like a deprivation. But in time you will come to see how this in fact expands your inner world, rather than diminishes it. In this, we are all privileged. By the end of this year you will have forged such self-confidence, such independence, all of which comes about in your learning of the practical ways of life. And as Professor Duncan himself said, Silver Creek's greatest gift is that it sometimes gives us the chance to see the vision of God in his Creation.'

There's singing after this, and another reading. Then Father Wilson performs the Holy Communion. I'm one of the few Red House girls not to rise and move towards the altar. As the next pew stands, and the next, I see that most of the school is heading down the aisle for their fill of the body and blood of Christ, and wonder if I am missing out on some crucial spiritual nourishment. What would happen if one evening I knelt at the altar and had a white tab placed on my tongue and sipped at the challis? I think of my parents, and swiftly feel a lurch of longing for home. I still haven't had a letter from them. Have they forgotten about me?

~

Later, back at the house preparing for bed, I hear a howl. I throw down my book and run out of the dorm. In the tog room I find Ronnie standing in front of a locker, a grotty garment dangling from the end of the broom she's holding.

'They *stink*!' she cries, pinching her nose with her forefinger. 'Kendall pissed her *pants*!'

They're the shorts Kendall had been wearing on the hike. Girls start talking over the top of each other, no one thinking to ask how Ronnie found them. Suddenly Kendall bursts in and Ronnie drops the broom.

We all watch as Kendall gathers the soggy shorts into a ball. She looks up, just once, and the expression on her face makes me think of an animal caught in a cage. Then she rushes away through the study in the direction of the deck.

'What's going on here?'

Briohny has wandered into the tog room, hands on her hips. Her grin is triumphant.

4
~

The next day, after lunch, hike groups are pinned to the noticeboard. We're heading off on our first overnight hike tomorrow, even though it is only midweek. Our weekends are now scheduled on Wednesdays and Thursdays, to avoid any crowds at the campsites and on the hike tracks.

Ronnie comes up beside me, putting a hand on my back to squint at the lists. 'Hey, Becky,' she says. 'We're in a group together.'

She calls to Portia, pointing at the board. Portia saunters over, throwing an arm around my shoulder. She smells like Dove. It's the three of us in the group, and another girl, Phoebe, from Orange House.

'Best group or what?' Portia says, pinching my waist.

Watching her walk up the stairs with Ronnie, my insides begin to bubble excitedly. I'll have two whole days with them.

We'll have loads of chats, loads of laughs, and then, by the end, we'll be firm friends. I just know it.

~

We set off late the next afternoon, the sun still blazing across the sky. The route takes us through a small neighbouring vineyard and a B&B, and then across meadows flushed with buttercups. Phoebe marches ahead, with Portia, and I walk at Ronnie's side. I've hardly spoken to Phoebe this afternoon—her family, I've heard, is *actually* friends with the Queen.

It's flat terrain, but there's no shade and we're all sweating heavily. We finally spot a giant gum in the middle of a paddock and stop for a drink. The girls slump to the ground, packs still strapped to their backs. Phoebe sits off to one side, gulping from her aluminium water bottle.

It isn't long before we reach camp at Daisy Creek. We find a site near the water, other girls' tents pitched on either side. The boys' campground is further away, across another road, near a toilet block. 'Pretty extreme version of the one-metre rule,' Ronnie sighs.

After Ronnie and I set up our tent, we wander down to the creek to collect fresh water. We splash about and I spot a yabbie. Portia makes jaffles for dinner, and later she disappears into the boys' area, where her voice somehow carries across the campsite.

When she comes back, we're already tucked up in our sleeping bags inside the tent. But she hauls us out. Phoebe is in the next tent, but Portia doesn't wake her.

'I want to tell you a story,' she says, stoking the fire. 'A *ghost* story.'

'Oooh,' says Ronnie.

Portia waves away the smoke. 'This is a story my grandad told me, from when he was on the cattle farm in Queensland, before he retired and sold up. He was on his own in the house one night, this big old homestead with a verandah that stretches all the way around, when he heard a knock on the door. *Funny*, he thinks. *It's a bit late for visitors.* So he doesn't answer. But there's another knock, then a bang. *Bang. Bang. Bang.* Now he's bothered. He grabs his shotgun, the one he keeps in the cupboard under the stairs, but when he opens the front door, barrel raised, no one's there.'

'Creepy,' Ronnie breathes.

'Well,' says Portia, licking her lips, 'by now my grandad doesn't know what to do. He thinks about ringing the cops, but the nearest police station is more than two hours' drive away—this is a huge station, there's no one around for miles. He closes the front door and goes back through to the sitting room, where he's got the fire going. Then the banging starts up again. *Bang. Bang. Bang.*'

'I'm scared now,' Ronnie says. 'No, really, this is scary.'

Portia nods, glancing at me. 'Wait,' she says. 'So Grandad's like, *This is fucked.* He grabs the shotgun again and marches to the front door. But on his way, he passes a big set of windows that during the day open out to the verandah. And there he sees it—an old woman, dressed in rags, with her face pressed against the glass.'

'No! He didn't!'

'By now he's packing himself—and I can tell you, it takes a lot to frighten my grandad. I mean, he was in the war. But he's shaking. He's got the gun, he runs to the front door, but when he opens it she's not there.'

'Where is she?' I croak.

They both look at me.

'She's sitting on the far fence,' Portia says. 'A hundred metres away—there's a big old lamppost near the tree—and she's laughing. *How did she get over there?* Grandad's wondering. *She was at the window only a few seconds ago.* And before he knows what he's doing, before he's really thought it through, he's raised the shotgun and fired at her. Now let me tell you: my grandad could hit an apple off your head a mile off—he is a plum shot. But you know what he saw? He could hardly believe his eyes. The bullet had gone *through* this woman. Right through her! He doesn't know what else to do but run back inside and slam the front door. Now my grandad's not religious but he was thinking this is the world's end, she's the devil, it's the apocalypse; the whole shebang.

'He doesn't open that front door all night. He doesn't move from the chair in front of the fire. But there's no more banging on the front door, and at first light he walks outside and makes his way towards the fence. The old woman's body is nowhere to be seen. But what he does find, on top of the fence post, is the bullet, aimed back towards the house.'

'No,' Ronnie moans. 'But where was the old woman?'

'She was a ghost,' I say. 'An apparition.'

Portia nods, holding my eye.

'Well that's fucked up,' says Ronnie. 'Thanks, Portia. There goes sleep tonight.'

We start to pack up around the fire, moving food and our cooking utensils back inside the tent. Portia drifts around camp silently, her shadow stretching long across the grass.

'Was that true, then?' I ask, throwing dirt on the smouldering coals. 'The story your grandfather told. Did you believe him?'

Portia just shrugs. 'Why wouldn't I believe him?' she says.

~

The next day is cooler as the sun lingers behind the clouds. We follow the trail along the creek before it veers deeper into the forest. It's dense and lush in here, the path overgrown in parts. There are ferns everywhere—some as tall as people. Portia picks blackberries from a ravine and rubs the fruit all over her face, staining it purple. We can't stop laughing, which makes her laugh too, until she can hardly breathe. I take a photo.

After a couple of hours, Portia suggests we run the rest of the way. 'We can get back to school sooner,' she reasons. 'Be the first girls in.'

I glance at Ronnie. I don't want to run. I've got a stomach ache; I need to go to the toilet, I've needed to for ages, but I don't want to take the trowel so the others know I'm doing a poo.

'Bec?' Portia says, in a voice that suggests it is my decision.

'Sure,' I say. 'Let's do it.'

It's a painful two hours. We jog on and off, our packs bouncing, our legs buckling whenever the path dips. My stomach grows tight like the skin of a barrel. I start to feel a bit sick, and have to stop once or twice, wincing as I lean against a tree.

'Are you okay?' Ronnie asks.

'Almost home,' Portia calls from the front. And we are—we hit the school drive twenty minutes later and are the first girls' group to sign back in. It feels good, being the first back. Being the fastest. The best.

'See?' Portia says as we walk back up to the house. 'I told you running was a good idea, didn't I?'

She stops on the track outside the chapel, her eyebrows raised. When I nod, she smiles again, but before I can say anything she has turned her back on me, continuing up the hill.

~

I wait until everyone else has showered before using the toilet. Then I have a long shower. Nothing, I think as I wash my hair and scrub at my arms and legs, has ever felt so good. Through the bathroom windows I hear other girls returning, someone stomping out into the boiler room to jam a few logs into the fire.

Wrapped in a towel, I wander back out to the dorm. There are a few more girls sprawled across their beds, still dressed in their filthy hiking gear. As I head towards my bed, I catch sight of Portia from the corner of my eye, prancing up and down the aisle naked.

I wait for others to laugh. But the dorm is silent. I scuttle to my bed, trying not to look at her white bum and breasts. She brings out a giant tub of talcum powder, begins tapping it against her underarms and pubic hair, then spreads herself across the bed like a model posing for a portrait, gazing around the dorm as if daring us to speak.

No one does, of course. I'm shocked at her brazenness—I usually get changed in the bathroom, or the toilet cubicles. Now I scramble to dress myself, towel caught under my arms, tugging on my pants and my crop top.

As I do, Ronnie stops at the foot of my bed. 'Your back is a bit spotty, dear,' she announces.

Now girls laugh. I hunch over, staring at the floor. *Why did she say that?* The spots come and go like a rash. I wanted to see the doctor about it but Mum would only buy me antiseptic wipes, and I feel a sudden jab of hatred towards her.

~

The next morning Portia draws me aside after breakfast. She wants to put up a clothesline out the back of the house. 'We'll do it together,' she says. 'Our own private project.'

Ronnie and Briohny have turned around, watching us fall back behind the group. That warm excitement returns, bubbling away in my stomach. How thrilling to be chosen by her, out of all the others.

'I'd love that,' I say.

She squeezes my arm. 'Awesome.'

We set to work that afternoon, clearing the bracken beneath the trees. We find a few planks of wood and some tough string, and it doesn't take long for her to fashion a working line. She doesn't really need me in the end, so while she hammers the nails into the trunk, I plant some grass seeds out the front of the house. The earth is hard and dry, but I toil until I've shaped a small channel, giving the earth a drink from the hose.

Portia reminds me of Serena, a girl I knew in my first year of primary school. They have the same dark hair, same freckles and colouring, except where Portia's eyes are sharp and narrow, Serena's were round and crinkly. Serena had been in grade six, and during the first weeks of term she was also my reading buddy. Every Wednesday I would meet her in the assembly room and read with her for an hour. I adored Serena. I wanted her to come home and live with me so we could go down to the beach every day and kick the football to one another.

That was until the afternoon she told me she couldn't be my buddy anymore because the program had finished, and I had curled my small fingers into a fist and belted her square on her back. I remember the sound so distinctly—a hollow thump—and her look of utter surprise. Not anger, or pain. I was sent back to my classroom, where the teacher made me stand in the corner. When Mum came to collect me, she wiped the hair from my brow and asked, 'Now why did you do that?'

After the gardening, Portia and I take a break out on the deck, sucking at our water bottles. The single cloud in the sky drifts across the sun. The dorm will be hot now, and stuffy. 'Can't believe we still don't have curtains,' Portia mutters.

I gaze down at Yellow House, shrouded in darkness. Most nights our dorm is awash with moonlight. There is little privacy, either—from the road you can see us getting changed if we stand too close to the windows.

'We'll get them,' I say.

Portia stares at me evenly, and shrugs.

But we never do. Day after day we complain, but Miss Lacey never does anything about it. I don't understand why she doesn't listen to us. Doesn't she care? Then one day she visits the house with sleeping masks, the kind you get on long-haul flights.

'Here you go,' she says, beaming as she hands them out. 'This should help at night.'

'This is instead of curtains?' I blurt out. 'Are you taking the piss?'

Her face grows dark. 'I won't be spoken to like that, Rebecca,' she says, and later I see she has marked me down for a detention—just like that.

'It's like *Animal Farm* here,' I grumble to Emma before lights-out. We've started reading it in English.

She looks up from her *Smash Hits* magazine and smiles. 'Only you would say that.'

~

Emma and I begin a photography elective. We learn how to develop black-and-white photos in a darkroom, and one afternoon we head out past the dam into the denser bush. I've got it in my head that I'll take wildlife photos, like David Attenborough, of butterflies and lizards and wallabies. But there aren't any animals around.

When we find a big tree with rope hanging from it, Emma sets up the camera on the tripod and takes snaps of me soaring across the canopy. 'Work it, work it,' she shouts in a silly British accent, which makes me laugh.

At dinner, I watch Emma with real fondness. She is kind to me in a way no one else in the house is—always complimenting me on my prep and telling me I am clever. I've never had a friend like that. She makes me feel good about myself. She doesn't seem to care whether other people like her or not; she doesn't try to talk to the country boys, and isn't interested in how long you've been at the school, or where you live. Emma lives in Mildura and she went to the local high school. She often talks about home, her brothers and sisters, and all her friends—she seems to have hundreds of them.

But some Red House girls don't like Emma. They call her a bogan because of her nasally voice. Emma doesn't mind. 'You're all a bunch of snobs,' she says good-naturedly. She always tells things like they are. I envy that about her, too. She doesn't want to be friends with Portia or Ronnie: 'They're just not *nice* girls,' she said to me once. I started to worry after that. *If she doesn't like them, what does she like about me?* If you strip me down, am I a *not-nice* girl too?

~

Another week goes by with no mail from my parents. It's been three weeks now, with no letters from home. I've written twice to Mum and Dad, telling them about the runs and the hikes. Why haven't they written back? Again I wonder if they've forgotten about me. It seems a ridiculous thought at first, but as the days stretch on, I begin to panic. *Maybe they're happier without me.*

One mail day I wait in the study with the girls as a young, plump Scottish assistant called Miss McKinney divvies out the post. 'Nothing for you, Starford,' she chuckles. 'Your parents enjoying themselves too much to write?'

It's only a joke but the words burn. 'Fat *fuck*,' I hiss after her, shocked at the venom in my voice. I turn and see Lou watching me from her desk, eyes wide.

Later that night, when everyone's in bed reading, I stay in the bathroom. I brush my teeth slowly, my feet growing cold on the tiles. Eventually I lock myself in a cubicle, where I stifle sobs with my T-shirt. Crying exhausts me, and I feel an odd weight of sadness, as though I'm both very old and very young.

5

Each night after dinner Lou and I climb on the roof to watch the sunset. 'My favourite part of the day,' says Lou, smiling at the shock of orange and pink across the sky. I think Lou misses home more than anyone. She always talks about it in a wistful way. Her parents are sheep farmers and they live on a property called The Plains, with cats and dogs and horses; she even has a pet lamb, named Molly.

Lou brings along letters to read. Mum has finally sent me two letters, which I keep in a box on my bedside table. There wasn't much to them—Mum wrote about how Archie bowled at cricket, and what video she and Dad watched on Saturday night. She didn't say why it had taken so long to write.

Up on the roof I can almost believe that the rest of the world has forgotten us. That we've slipped through some crack in time. Memories of home are fading and in their place have seeped the faces and voices and gestures of the girls, growing so familiar I know them better than my own.

But tonight, instead of heading to the roof after dinner, Lou and I set up a tent on top of Dusty Hill. It's Red House's turn for Fire Watch.

Lou and I take first shift, scanning the blue-black distance and making notes in the logbook. Bushfires are a real danger this time of year. Being out here makes me think about my parents. The year before I was born they lost everything in the Ash Wednesday fires. Their house was destroyed, along with Mum's car and most of their possessions.

'Even your clothes?' I once asked.

Mum looked away, at her cuticles. She doesn't like to talk about it.

'We had *nothing*,' she said at last. 'We went to work that morning and by evening everything was gone.'

I used to wonder how they managed to start again. To buy a new car to get to work, or buy appliances to cook dinner—all those things you need to exist. But now I'm at Silver Creek I realise you don't really need a lot of stuff in your life. I don't miss the comforts of home either—not television or Nintendo or the phone. I can cook all kinds of meals on a fire; I've washed myself in the river. You don't need many clothes, either—I've been wearing the same pair of jeans for weeks. There is something liberating about not feeling reliant on all those possessions, about not feeling attached.

We still get newspapers: each evening the *Herald Sun* and the *Age* are delivered to the house, where they lie in a stack next to the fireplace, gathering dust. No one ever wants to read them. What use is news of the outside world to us here?

But one night, out of curiosity, Simone and I open the front page to a story about Saddam Hussein and his chemical attacks on Kurdish people. It seems tensions in that region have been simmering again for some time.

Simone grows agitated, throwing the paper aside. 'You know what this means?' she says. 'The end of the world.'

Simone has always had a vivid imagination. Even so, I'm frightened. This is different from her other stories (like the white streak in her hair a result of being struck by lightning). This has secondary sources.

Over beef stroganoff, we describe our impending doom to the rest of Red House. Cities will be obliterated, millions will die. Silver Creek, Simone reasons, should escape the fallout longer than the cities, and when Saddam comes after us we can retreat to the bush. 'Just like Ellie in *Tomorrow, When the War Began*.' In her excitement Simone's post-war world becomes more and more fantastical: 'We'll live in the wombat burrows and survive on wild berries!'

When Miss Lacey visits the house during prep, Simone waves the newspaper at her, inviting me to outline the survival strategy. Miss Lacey reads the article, looks at us, and laughs and laughs until the whole study stares. 'I hate to disappoint you,' she says, 'but I don't think we're going to be invaded anytime soon. Still, it's a great story.'

Miss Lacey never takes us seriously. I reflect on this after she's gone, frowning as I slump over my desk. She visits the house less than she used to, and when she does she's always wary, searching our faces as if for some clue to a trick. It didn't matter to her that I was actually afraid. 'What if we *were* in real danger?' I say to no one in particular. 'Would she even believe us?'

I find Portia watching. 'Nah,' she murmurs. 'She doesn't care about us.'

'But it's her job.'

Portia shakes her head. 'She's no different from other teachers. Pretending to be nice but really not giving a shit.' She stares at the tip of her sneakers, her eyes dark. 'Maybe she needs a little test?'

~

A bloodcurdling scream brings Miss Lacey charging into the dorm the following night.

'What is it?' she cries. 'What's the matter?' Her torchlight bounces around the dark like a fly caught under glass.

I sit up, doona pulled high to my chin, the story ready: *I saw a man at the window.* But before I can speak the light drops to the floor and Miss Lacey sighs. 'Right,' she says. 'I see what's going on here.'

No one moves. No one says a word. Miss Lacey puts a hand on her hips, surveying the dorm. 'What?' she scoffs. 'Cat got your tongues now?'

'We saw a man,' I say. 'At the window. You . . .'

'Oh, just be quiet, Rebecca.'

She leans against the doorway and I can see she is dressed in a pretty blouse and jeans. Like she was going out, if there was anywhere to go up here.

'Enough of these pranks,' she says, steering the torchlight over each bed. 'Do you understand?' When she reaches me she pauses, and the light flares in my eyes. 'If I hear another sound,' she warns, 'I'll make sure you all sleep in tents for a week.'

I yank the doona over my head as her footsteps retreat along the road. I lie like this, amid the fusty air, until it becomes hard to breathe, clenching at the pillow until my hands ache. *Why doesn't she believe me?*

~

I'm still sulking on the way to breakfast the next morning when Portia appears next to me. She's got a story, she says, that will cheer me up. It's about a secret ritual at Silver Creek called the Bell Run. You run to the chapel in the middle of the night, she explains, ring the outside bell as many times as you dare, then run back to your house. 'And,' she says, a wicked glint in her eye, 'you have to do it *nude*.'

I laugh, but as I do I feel the colour rise to my face. I wonder if the others know about the Bell Run. It seems an odd sort of ritual—running around the bush in the middle of the night with no clothes on. I don't say it, of course, but I don't fancy getting naked in front of anyone.

A week later Portia again draws me aside. 'I want to do it,' she whispers. 'Tonight. You up for it?'

I hadn't thought she was serious, and for a moment I'm peeved with her. But Portia and I have been getting along so well, I don't want to spoil it now. I like being her friend; I like walking with her to breakfast, I like running with her on the crossies. I like the power I feel in her company; how the boys nod hello to me as I walk by. Most of all I like the way other girls look at me: with hesitation, with a bit of admiration. And with a bit of fear.

'I don't know,' I say.

We'll get in a lot of trouble if we're caught—detentions, or worse: Stoney Roads, a five-kilometre run to the bottom of the school drive and back at dawn.

'You scared?' Portia teases. 'Come on, it'll be fun.'

'Just the two of us?' I say, glancing around the dorm.

Portia shakes her head. 'Sarah's coming too. Actually,' she says with a smile, 'she suggested it.'

I raise my eyebrows. Sarah is a quiet girl who sleeps in the bed next to Briohny. Hardly the first person I'd think would suggest a Bell Run. Sarah's in my French class, though Ronnie doesn't like her—'Once a nerd, always a nerd,' she whispered at the start of term. I didn't know she and Portia were friends.

'All right,' I say. 'I'm up for it.'

That night, after lights-out, when Miss McKinney has headed back down the slope towards Yellow House, I meet Portia and Sarah in the tog room.

'So how do we do this, then?' I ask, running my hands up and down my goose-pimpled arms.

'I guess we just strip and sprint, yeah?' says Portia. We start giggling.

I edge my boxer shorts over my hips until they fall in a silky pile to the floor. Portia and Sarah both have their backs to me as they undress, Portia's white bum virtually glowing in the dark.

I hunch over as we make our way along to the road, absurdly trying to hide my breasts. Not that Sarah and Portia are looking—they're both walking ahead, tall, like tribal leaders on their way to battle. It's so quiet out here. The stars are sparkling like cut diamonds on a black cloth. I don't know what we'll do if someone comes across us. But there is no one around. The road is empty, the night is still, a crisp vacuum. The school is ours.

At the path, Portia waves us towards some bushes. Her arm brushes against mine and it feels like a current of electricity along my skin. I've never been so close to another naked girl. I try not to look at either of them, fixing my eyes to the ground. But when the moon drifts out from behind the clouds I have a full view of Sarah's brown, fleshy breasts and the mass of dark hair between her legs. She's like a full-grown woman, and I frown down at my own flat chest.

Crouched there, Portia's eyes dart about. 'We'd better get a move on,' she whispers, nodding towards the bell. 'Bags not first.'

'Bags not second,' Sarah breathes.

They both look at me, grinning.

'Fuck's sake,' I mutter.

The rope is smooth and cool in my hands. After a deep breath, I give a tug. But it's heavier than I expected and the bell comes out sounding more like a pencil rattling in a tin. The girls snigger from the bushes, and Portia says, 'Pull it harder!' I tug again, with all my weight this time, and the bell tolls mournfully into the night.

Instantly they're on either side of me. Portia yanks the rope away, gives it a few tugs, Sarah after her. But I've already taken off, up the path and along the road. Some primal fear has taken over my legs; I can't stop running. My teeth are chattering so hard they feel like they might shatter.

The girls soon catch me up. We plough up the path, laughing, uncaring now about who hears. At the back door Portia pulls us into a hug. 'We did it!' she squeals. I feel my breast squash against Sarah's arm, her flesh hard and cold.

A few girls are sitting up, one or two beginning to clap, and I make a silly bow at the top of the aisle. As I move towards my bed, Portia reaches out, takes hold of my wrist. 'Well done, mate,' she says.

~

When I wake the next morning I feel different. I throw off the covers and get dressed, humming a tune under my breath.

'You're chirpy,' Emma mutters as we stand at opposite basins, brushing our teeth. Portia strolls past, towards the toilet cubicle, and in the mirror she winks at me.

I practically run to breakfast. I feel taller, stronger. On the way into the dining hall, a girl from Yellow House calls out, 'Hey, Rebecca, is it true—did you do the Bell Run?'

There is a teacher nearby, and he turns to me, eyes narrowed. The Yellow House table are all staring at me now, waiting.

Normally I hate to be looked at like this; I will blush and slump and mumble. But everything has changed—this feeling isn't shame or embarrassment. It's thrilling.

'I think we're busted,' Portia murmurs through a mouthful of Corn Flakes. On the teachers' table Miss Lacey is talking with the headmaster, Mr Pegg, occasionally glancing our way.

'But how could she know?' Sarah says.

'Someone dobbed,' I suggest.

Portia shakes her head. 'Nah. Who'd have the guts to do that?'

But after breakfast we're summoned to Mr Pegg's office. He makes us stand in a line in front of his desk while he drones on about the dangers of being out of bounds at night. Boys, he scolds, could have come across us. 'Or worse,' he says, 'a hermit.'

Mr Pegg is a stooping man with a deep voice, but up close his face is strangely childlike, round and soft at the edges.

He gives us each a Stonely Road. He points a thin, bloodless finger at me. 'And you, Rebecca,' he says, 'will be first.'

Back at the house, we stand at the entrance to the dorm and give each other a high-five. 'Stonely Roads, ladies,' Portia calls like a game-show host, and everyone cheers. Sarah and Portia seem genuinely thrilled with their punishment, but I'm more subdued. I wonder if my parents will be told about the Bell Run. I hope not.

Apart from Simone, no one in the house knows about my scholarship. So they don't really know what's at stake each time I get in trouble. Dad won't be happy if he finds out. He's a high-school principal and strict with my brother and me, always expecting better from us, no matter the circumstance. But how could he ever understand what it's like up here? Then I feel a surge of shame. My parents are already giving up so much for me to be at Silver Creek; even with the scholarship the fees are enormous. More, I know, than they can afford.

It is still dark when I get out of bed, the moon cutting slivers of light through the wall. I drag myself from under the covers and, so as not to wake anyone, get changed in the tog room, my feet like iceblocks on the tiles.

Out the front of the library a Jeep rumbles in the dark, white exhaust spewing from the back. I can't see anyone else around, not even Rich Browne, who I've heard has Stonely Roads most mornings.

I'm about to sit on the steps when a voice from deep within the Jeep shouts, 'What are you waiting for, Rebecca? You've got thirty-five minutes.'

The descent seems to take forever. I can still hardly see a thing, tripping and skidding on loose stones. The bush leans in towards the road, menacing. I hear the crackle and snap of things moving about in the shrubs, and fear starts to seep into my blood, turning it cold. My breath is noisy, as though amplified out here. This isn't so much fun, after all.

To make sure I don't walk the Jeep follows me, its headlights casting a long shadow across the road. Near the bottom my laces come loose and I crouch to tie them. My eyes are streaming. The Jeep rolls up behind and blasts its horn, which gives me such a fright I lose my balance and keel over. I lie on the road like an overturned beetle until the disembodied voice hollers from the window, 'Don't you dare stop running!'

I turn my head, miserable, and stare right at the lights. They're like two burning suns in a black sky.

Later that morning my class goes swimming at the dam. I dress in board shorts and a T-shirt: in my bathers I feel shy around the other girls from other houses, which seems strange to me after I had the guts to get nude for the Bell Run. The water is tea-coloured and the mud on the bottom squelches beneath my toes. I try not to think about snakes lurking in the reeds. A few girls dive from the board and I watch their slender figures rise in the air and plunge into the water.

I float on my back, away from the others, the sun hot against my face. Murky shapes glide across my eyelids. I can't hear anything, floating like this. I can only feel the bob of the water, the breeze brushing against my forehead. I close my eyes. I'm so tired after the Stonely Road, but the splash of the boys' bombs into the dam makes me flinch.

I feel on edge for the rest of the morning, and at lunch, as I'm handing my crockery back to the slushie, I drop my plate. It crashes to the floor and the entire dining hall roars, banging their fists on their tables, as is the custom. Immediately I feel my face flush and my hands begin to shake. Somehow I hold in my tears.

Later, on the way back up to the house after class, Lou loops her arm through mine and urges me around the back, where there's an old fruit box near the door. We drag it around to the top of the dusty slope. Lou sits at the front, her legs bunched up around her face, while I sit behind, my legs hanging over the sides. We push off, tunnelling through a flume of hot air, laughing all the way down.

At the bottom Lou tries to get out but she's stuck, and by now we're both howling. Then I feel something warm gush between my legs and an earthy pong rises like steam. Piss is pooling in the box. It's everywhere, creeping towards Lou.

My ears roar with a rabid panic. Girls are gathering at the top of the slope to watch. Finally Lou climbs out, kicking up another mushroom of dust. Only when she's a few paces up the slope do I tip myself out. There's now a puddle of piss in the dirt, and I grind it under my heel before scurrying across the sand towards the deck, away from the others, dragging the box along with me.

'What are you doing?'

Lou is staring down at me, shielding her face from the sun.

'Just looking for a new box.' I tug at my soaked shorts. 'This is breaking apart.'

Lou stares a moment longer. Then she gives a wave and carries on up the slope.

I run to a bathroom cubicle and slump against the toilet seat. My whole body is shaking. Am I so nervous around everyone that I can't control my bladder? What if Briohny finds out? I can't bear to think about it.

I don't know how long I stay like this, my head on my knees, but eventually I hear the girls' voices grow dim as everyone drifts down the hill for dinner.

~

During prep, Portia calls me over to her desk. She has her sketchpad out to show me some drawings. Portia can draw anything—faces, landscapes, dream worlds. Sometimes she invites me to join her on the deck, where we sip on cups of raspberry cordial and eat Saladas. We've also been into the bush at the back of the house, where she smokes a cigarette and we fossick among the foliage. Other times we sit on the edge of her bed to look at her photos. She likes to show me the same ones over and over. They're mostly of her mum. She lives in Queensland with her girlfriend. Portia stays with them on holidays.

Portia doesn't even mind that her mum is gay. No one in the house teases her about it. I've never heard of anyone's mum being gay. How does that even work? Was she always gay, or did she change her mind about men when she was with Portia's dad? I don't know any gay women, but my dad used to work with a man who lived with another man in an apartment near the city. His name was Tim, and he wore a gold earring and looked a bit like Elton John, who was also once married to a woman. It's all very confusing.

These men used to have dinner parties where Mum and Dad drank lots of wine while Archie and I watched videos upstairs, sprawled across the soft leather couches. The apartment was spotless and everything seemed to match. I liked the bathroom best, with its heat lamps and enormous bathtub, always smelling like the spicy cologne Dad occasionally wears to work.

When I look at Portia I think of Tim. They're both poised, confident in their appearance, in their *look*. With her Mooks sweaters and old jeans worn at the knee, Portia has the best clothes of all the girls at Silver Creek. The only thing I like in my drawers is a Quicksilver T-shirt I bought for myself at Christmas.

Portia has endless stories about camping trips, race meets in Armidale, tennis tournaments at Blairgowrie, long hot summers on Fraser Island. Her older brothers supply the booze, and she's hooked up with heaps of boys. She's even given Rollo Walker, the best-looking guy in the school, a blowjob.

'You'll have to come stay with me in Queensland,' she says casually one afternoon. 'Best beaches in the world. We eat prawns and lobster every day. It's awesome.'

Imagine going to Queensland to stay with Portia! I feel big and smug to have been singled out, to have been picked above all the rest. But I try not to show too much excitement. Portia, after all, is fickle. One day she likes someone, the next day she doesn't—that much I have learnt about her. Only this morning, on the way back from chapel, she told me that she doesn't like many girls in the house.

We had taken the long route behind the art school. Smoke from the burn-off in the front paddocks tickled my throat.

'Red House are just sheep,' she said, reaching for a stick lying beside the path. 'Always following. It's so *boring*.'

'But some are all right,' I said. 'I mean, what about Ronnie?'

Portia didn't reply. She slashed at some wattle.

I stopped. 'What about me?' I was trying to be light-hearted, but I could hear the plea in my voice. I wonder if Portia could hear it too.

'I'm not sure,' she said finally, after giving me an even stare. 'I haven't worked you out yet.'

That evening it is too humid to sleep. Portia and I go out to the deck and begin throwing stones on Yellow House's roof. We have a system—three throws each while the other keeps guard, taking breaks for a sip on a glass of cool milk. The stones on the tin sound like gunfire.

~

Miss Lacey leads a group to collect firewood. We forage in the scrub at the back of the house, gathering up bracken, kindling, and larger branches and logs. It's overcast, the air clotted. We have already made about half-a-dozen trips to the boiler room when my back begins to seize up.

'How long are we doing this?' moans Briohny.

'Come on,' Miss Lacey calls. 'If you get enough now, you won't run out later in the term.'

'Who the fuck *cares*?' Sarah mutters, a large log balanced between us. 'Why don't we just have a hot-water system?'

Ronnie was wrong about Sarah: she's changed since our Bell Run. No longer the compliant, well-behaved one, she talks loudest after lights-out, and smokes in the boiler room every afternoon.

I like Sarah. She has wonderful stories about Indonesia, where her family lives, describing the food and heat and the local people in vivid detail. I have seen photos of her brother stuck to the wall beside her bed. He looks like a female version of Sarah, with the same bad skin and upturned nose. He smokes a lot of pot, Sarah once said. 'So much that he sees things. Dragons in the sky and giant mushrooms blooming from the ground.'

We stagger through the trees until Sarah trips on a root, sending the log flying. As we lean over to pick it up, Sarah nods towards Miss Lacey and whispers, 'Look.' Miss Lacey is bent over with a sack of kindling and beneath her grey sweatpants is the clear outline of a g-string. We snigger until she spins around.

'What is it?'

Sarah throws a smirk my way, glancing back at Miss Lacey beneath her dark lashes. '*Well* . . .' she says, 'we were just admiring your g-string.'

The log strains in my arms. Miss Lacey blinks, fixing her eyes on Sarah, then me, and there's something in her face I haven't seen before: contempt.

'What a stupid thing to say,' she snaps. 'I'll be seeing you both in detention.'

She stalks back through the trees. Sarah laughs, dropping the log into a damp patch of earth. I watch Miss Lacey go, shame prickling at my fingertips. *Turn back.* But she doesn't and I kick at a pile of old leaves.

'What's the matter?' Sarah asks as I look over my shoulder. Miss Lacey is gone.

~

It's prep. I should be at my desk. Instead I'm in the bathroom, running cold water over my hand, which I burnt on the boiler.

Back in the study I find Miss Lacey at my desk, turning over a page in my workbook.

'Yes?' I say, scraping my chair across the floor and sitting down.

She looks up from the workbook. 'Where were you?'

I shrug.

'Rebecca?'

'I was in the bathroom, okay. What's the big deal?'

She slaps her palm against the desk. 'That's it. Go to the boiler room. Go on, get out.'

'What the hell? Why?'

'I said *get out*!'

Her face has gone white, her pupils like pinpricks. Everyone in the study turns to look—it's the first time Miss Lacey has shouted like this.

I storm outside, but she follows, grabbing at my arm. We're almost tussling.

'This is bullshit!' I cry.

'I *beg* your pardon? What is the *matter* with you?'

'I burnt my hand! But you don't care about that, do you?'

Miss Lacey shakes her head. 'I'm getting pretty sick and tired of all this, Rebecca—you need to work on your attitude. Think about what's at stake here every time you open your mouth for some snide remark, all right? You can stay out here and think about your behaviour.'

I slump into the plastic seat beside the woodbin. Under the lurid light I see how dark circles bruise her eyes, her hair frizzing at her temples like a girl's—and I remember that she isn't that much older than me, maybe twenty-five or twenty-six.

'What are you smirking at?'

I shrug. 'Nothing.'

She nods a few times, chewing on her lip. It looks like she's going to say something, maybe try to get to the bottom of whatever is going on here. Part of me wants that—for her to like me again. But then I think, Why should I have to make it up to her? I haven't done anything wrong. Blowing air from my lips, I ask how long I have to stay out in the cold. 'You know,' I sneer, 'I don't want to get *pneumonia*.'

Her face hardens. 'You'll stay out here all bloody night if you have to.'

When she's gone I slump further into the seat, tracing my sneaker up and down the boiler. I like it out here, on my own. I can hear myself think, and I can think about anything I want. But all I can think about is Miss Lacey and her anger. It was thrilling, to see her upset—because of me.

Later that night I can't sleep. My hand stings hot beneath the sheets. I get up a few times to run it under more water. This only eases the pain for a few minutes and I end up sleeping with my hand pressed against the metal bedstead.

I dream Miss Lacey is chasing me. We're thrashing through the bush out the back of the house, the sun high in the sky. She is shouting unintelligibly at me, and I'm terrified—a cold, black fear. In the long grass by the dam she catches me and her nails dig sharp at my skin.

~

The next night, when everyone else is asleep, Emma and I creep off to the tuck room for a Milo. As Emma pours milk into her mug, she asks, 'Why do you always suck up to Portia?'

'What?'

'You shouldn't, you know. The other girls like you already. They look up to you.'

I almost laugh, but in the gloom I can see Emma is frowning. 'No they don't,' I say.

She shrugs. 'Maybe,' she says, reaching for the light, 'you shouldn't worry so much what other people think.'

I stay out there in the dark. So that's where I stand on the spectrum of our friendship: on the cusp of potential, but only if I become better, nicer. It's a painful thought, almost like betrayal, and I ball my hands into fists, squeezing at a sudden fury towards Emma. 'Like it's that *easy*,' I want to shout.

At the window in the corner the moon shines dully at the opaque glass. I think of Father Wilson and his sermon. About how Silver Creek gives us the chance to see God in his Creation. But it isn't that; it isn't that at all. You don't see anything clearer up here: not the girls in the house, the teachers, or whatever god there might be. You only see yourself, stripped back, bare. You see yourself in an unflinching light, and you cannot look away.

6
~

The more I think about Kendall, the more intrigued I am. She can't help but stand out in a drab dorm with brown walls and a brown floor—her hair is so very white. And those eyes, such an intense blue; they almost radiate from her pale face, as do her blood-red lips. There is something ethereal about her, like she lived a whole other life before this one.

But what I notice most about Kendall is how much time she spends on her own. Trailing behind on the way to breakfast, or sitting on her bed after school. I feel sorry for her; she must be lonely. But after a while I see that she doesn't mind this solitude; in fact I think she rather likes it. After class she heads back to the house along the service track, on her own but at a relaxed pace, almost a stroll. She may not chime in with all the chatter, but she is always listening, even when she appears not to be—I often catch her smiling at snatches of talk around the dorm.

I wonder if she has any friends outside of Red House. I've seen her talking after class to the girls from her slow hike group. Perhaps they are all friends. But here in the house she barely talks to anyone. How does she manage it, surrounded by so many people? I've never seen her get sad or angry. How does she preserve that discipline of feelings? I almost admire her for it.

One afternoon I find myself alone in the dorm with her and we strike up a conversation about fencing. It turns out Kendall is good at fencing, with a high ranking in the Victorian league. Just as I'm picturing her jousting in medieval castles, the rest of the house returns like a stampede, and when Ronnie overhears she suggests Kendall must look like the Michelin Man in her fencing costume, which makes everyone laugh.

From across the aisle I fume at Ronnie. I had been enjoying our chat. Kendall's face is expressionless, but I do catch something beseeching in her eyes. I know I should say something, stand up for her, but an instant later that look is gone.

~

It isn't long after this that Kendall begins snoring. And it isn't dainty snoring, as I discover the first night, but congested rumbles that seem to shake the very foundations of the house. When girls complain, Kendall says it isn't her. Slippers get thrown, and Sarah even flings a hiking boot, striking Kendall in the head.

'I can't help it,' Kendall says.

One night, as I chat quietly to Emma after lights-out, I notice a figure in the shadows beside my bed. I scream. But it's only Kendall, holding a pillow. Her face looks strange, like she's underwater. Her eyes are blank.

'If you don't shut up,' she whispers, 'I'll smother you with my pillow.'

'Woah, Kends,' says Emma. 'Calm down.'

'If you don't shut up,' she says again, turning her cold gaze on Emma, 'I'll smother you *both* with my pillow.'

The girls around us laugh as Kendall edges away, propping the pillow against her bedside table.

I watch Kendall warily after that, no longer sure what she is capable of. I had thought we might get along—we'd never be friends, of course, but we could at least be civil to one another, have the occasional chat like the one we had about fencing. Now something is broken, and any compassion I might have felt for her has disappeared.

For others, Kendall's nocturnal outburst is the ammunition they have been waiting for all term. Ronnie, in particular, seizes any opportunity to be cruel. She hounds Kendall, pointing, jeering, sometimes even pushing her, for crimes like walking during crossies, or stinking out the bathroom. More of Kendall's smelly clothes are exhumed and paraded around the dorm.

Even Kendall's diary is plucked from her desk, with Ronnie reading out the choice bits to whoever will listen. Like the passage about Kendall tricking the teachers into believing she fainted on a hike: '*And then I slumped to my knees and pretended to fall. Haha, it was so easy, they didn't even check if I was unconchus.* You can't even spell,' Ronnie laughs. 'You spaz.'

And I am always there, at Ronnie's side, laughing with her. No one stands up to us. Even Kendall doesn't bother to defend herself—she just sits on the end of her bed, never uttering a word. But it doesn't feel mean like it might have before, because Kendall scared me. I didn't do anything to her; it was unprovoked. She needs to be punished for that. Taught a lesson.

One time, however, she does fight back. It's morning and I'm turning down my bed. The house has failed inspection again, so I must make sure my area is tidy. As I smooth out my doona,

I become aware of girls mingling at the top of the aisle. Then I hear Kendall and Briohny, voices raised, nearer to the door. I look up to see Emma creeping up behind Kendall with the broom and poking her, quite playfully, in the bum. The girls begin to tussle, Emma laughing, but it is no game to Kendall. Her eyes have that blank look to them.

'Hey!' I shout as Kendall snatches the broom and smacks Emma on the chin.

Briohny starts shouting, calling her *stupid slut* and *bitch*. Kendall turns around, the handle gripped at her waist like barbells. She seems to size Briohny up, before storming down the aisle. She slams into her with the full force of the broom, catching Briohny around the windpipe and pinning her against the cupboard.

I scream, but Kendall is gone before I reach her, charging out the back door and up into the bush.

It's all over in half a minute, maybe less. Emma stares at the floor, rubbing at her chin.

'What the hell was that?' I gasp.

Later, when Miss Lacey inspects the house, I tell her Kendall went to the nurse. 'With a stomach ache,' I lie.

Kendall doesn't reappear until dinnertime. She sits hunched at the end of the table, picking at her meal. No one mentions the broom, or what happened in the dorm.

But Briohny doesn't forget. Each night she peers into the bathroom mirror to examine the bruise around her throat. 'I'll never forgive her,' she says. 'I mean, she could have killed me. Crazy bitch.' She glances at me accusingly.

I try not to listen to Briohny. About anything, really. It's difficult. Her voice always pierces the throng of noise in the house. I don't think I'll ever like Briohny. Her miserliness is the worst: I've never seen her give away a single piece of food or can of drink, or lend someone anything. Rather than keep her food in the tuck room like the rest of us, she hides it in a carpenter's toolbox beneath her bed.

This red box has a strange power over me. Imagining its contents can entertain me for hours. Already I've caught glimpses of chocolate bars, crackers and the occasional packet of dried meat her mum brings back from holidays to America. Briohny's always careful to lock the box before returning it to the drawer. 'Because you're all thieves,' she says.

The box is brought out after every crossie. Sprawling the length of her bed, Briohny sucks on a can of Coke, stuffing crisps into her mouth. When she's finished she throws the packet, rather lavishly, to the floor.

Today I wander over and ask if I might have a chip. A few girls are getting changed; others lie on their beds, waiting for showers.

'No,' Briohny says. Stray bits of hair dance about her ears like sea anemone.

'Not one chip, Briohny?' I ask, loud enough for everyone to hear. 'You won't give me a single chip?'

She stabs a salty finger at me. 'No,' she says, her voice rising to a shout. 'No, no, no! They're mine. Mine! You're nothing but a scab, Bec. You hear me? A scab! Why don't you just *go away*?'

Stunned, I shuffle back to my bed, a few giggles pinging around the dorm.

The next afternoon my viola lesson finishes early and I come back to the house before everyone else. As I throw myself across my bed, I catch a flash of fire engine red. Briohny's tuck box has been left out on her quilt, key still in the lock. It doesn't seem possible. This has never happened before. I glance at my watch: the girls won't be back for at least ten minutes.

I creep over to Briohny's corner and sit on the edge of her quilt. I run my fingertips over the box's cool lacquered surface before tipping open the lid to expose the mass of treasure—more wonderful than I'd ever imagined. The box is stuffed with bars of chocolate, jellybeans, lollipops, Starbursts and ten-packs of Wizz Fizz. But all I can see is the packet of Lay's Cheese Onion just sitting there on top of the pile.

I rip it open and stuff a handful of chips into my mouth. I shower her quilt in crumbs, and when I finish I throw the packet on the floor.

'You stole them, didn't you?'

Briohny stands at the end of my bed. She's clasping her dog-eared Japanese textbooks tight in her arms.

I put my own book to one side. 'What are you talking about?'

'I know it was you,' she says. 'No one else has been up here.'

My tongue nudges at the chips stuck in my back teeth. 'Briohny,' I say, 'I didn't steal them. Why would I?'

'Because that's what you're like!' She is yelling now, her face right up close to mine, spidery veins creeping across her cheeks.

I lie back, smiling; I can't help it.

'You just have to have everything, don't you?' she says, kicking at my drawer. 'Why don't you just admit it, you fucking hypocrite.'

Later that night, watching Briohny and Portia laughing, I turn over a sour taste in my mouth. Why does Portia like her so much? Maybe she appreciates Briohny's bleak outlook on life. Or maybe it isn't that at all, I think, grabbing a towel. Maybe it's because Briohny doesn't try to make anyone like her.

I'm still thinking about this when I get back from class one afternoon to find Ronnie and Portia lingering in the corner of the dorm. They're both dressed in crossie gear, headbands pulling their eyes wide.

'Bec!' Ronnie blocks my way. 'Want to know Kendall's new nickname?'

Kendall is crouched next to her bed, sorting through her drawers.

'Okay,' I say.

'*KFC.*'

I frown. 'Like the chicken?'

Ronnie glances at Portia, then lets out a shrill laugh.

'It stands,' Portia says, 'for Kendall's Fat Cunt.'

For a moment the dorm seems to pitch, and I reach out to steady myself against the bed. As I do, I see behind Portia how Kendall's shoulders drop, her head slumping forward like it is too heavy for her neck. Ronnie has her hands on her knees, laughing so hard tears stream down her face. But Portia watches on unsmiling, her jaw flexing against her cheek.

I edge away. 'That's so mean,' I whisper.

Portia spins around. '*What?*' She grabs at my arm, pulling me towards her, so near I can see the tiny beads of sweat above her lip. 'What did you say, Rebecca?'

'Nothing,' I say, shrugging her off.

'KFC,' Ronnie wheezes. 'Classic.'

When they've gone I pace the length of the dorm. Everything is tight and achy. I should relish this time in the house on my own, but instead I am queasy, a deep black feeling, sticky as tar. I go to the window and press my nose against the cool glass. I'm looking for something, I just don't know what.

7
~

The next day Portia doesn't save me a seat in the dining hall. Briohny sits in my place, her face squished against her fists as she stares morosely at the casserole served up from the trolley. *It's nothing,* I tell myself. *You can't sit with her every meal.*

But I catch Portia watching me through lunch. Her eyes narrow for a moment, but she always smiles, toothless and tight.

Later that night I come across her and Briohny whispering in the tuck room. They fall silent when I walk in, and I feel their eyes on the back of my head as I rummage about in my locker. I find my Monte Carlos and draw one from the plastic sheath.

'What's up?' I say, trying to keep my voice calm.

More silence, until Portia says, 'We're thinking of dorm raiding Yellow House tonight. You interested?'

I turn around. Briohny is easy to read, her feelings like words on her face. She looks smug, standing there with her arms folded, as though she's worked out the answer to an equation before anyone else. I'm not so sure about Portia. The corner of her mouth is twitching, but her eyes are cold. I fold my own arms to stop them trembling. Portia is still staring at me, waiting for an answer. I feel like I've been given a handful of priceless sand that's now slipping through my fingers.

'Who else is coming?' I ask, biting into the biscuit.

The Monte Carlos have gone stale, the cream in the middle slightly sour, and I throw the rest of it in the bin.

'Me and Bri,' Portia says. 'And Sarah, too.'

I've already had Stonely Roads for being out of bounds. How far can I push Miss Lacey and Mr Pegg before I start to get in serious trouble, where my parents are involved and my scholarship is at risk? But I also really want to go. It'll be fun, and a bit dangerous. And I don't want to miss out on doing this with Portia. She will like me more, after the dorm raid; we'll become firmer friends. It's too good an opportunity to miss.

'Okay,' I say. 'I'm in.'

Portia glances at Briohny and claps her hands. 'Nice one, mate,' she says.

She saunters by, giving my shoulder a squeeze, and I smile back weakly. I can't work out why Briohny is still sneering from the corner of the room.

~

The moon is high and bright in the sky. Red House seems so small from the road, so far away.

We enter through the back door, tiptoeing across the cool tiles like a SWAT team. Yellow House is a carbon copy of Red House, but it smells more cold and clean; it's a lemony smell, mixed with pine. In the dorm, I creep, as planned, towards a bed in the middle. Lying under the covers is Freya. She's a nice girl, someone I would like to be friends with if I knew how. But it is too late; Portia has already bellowed, 'Dorm raid!'

Freya sits bolt upright and I slam the pillow across her face, knocking her back down with an *ooph*. When a few girls start to get out of bed, Sarah rushes at them, and screams mingle with our own crazed laughter.

At the top of the aisle Briohny tosses flour into the air, and for a few moments it's like being in a blizzard. Portia moves from one bed to the next, still lashing out with her oversized pillow. Her eyes shine like a cat's in the dark.

The whole thing lasts for about a minute before we're out the back door. 'That was awesome!' I cry, leaping up our front steps.

Briohny shoves me in the back. 'Shut the fuck up, Bec. Do you want the whole school to hear?'

~

The next morning, before the others are awake, I run to the bathroom to throw up. I barely slept a wink the night before, tossing and turning with worry. I stand over the toilet bowl, my legs quivering, and close my eyes. I don't want to be like this anymore. I want to be good again. I flush the toilet. *Please, God, don't let Dad find out.*

The others don't appear bothered about the trouble we're facing. Briohny is getting dressed with uncharacteristic joviality, and on the way down to breakfast I can hear Portia whistling.

Emma draws up beside me. 'Are you all right?'

My hands and brow are clammy. 'I didn't sleep well,' I mumble.

Emma tilts her head, still watching me, and I find myself blurting out my fears about losing my scholarship.

We walk past the chapel. 'But what's the big deal?' Emma asks. 'Why the secret? I'd love to tell people I'm smart enough to be on a scholarship.'

We stop at the bench. Soft light dapples through the trees. Emma puts her arm around me, which makes me happy and sad at the same time, because I know she knows that I don't want to be different. That I don't want anyone thinking I don't deserve to be here.

Birds skitter across the path. Some feed together on crusts of bread. I feel a pang of longing for my family, for my own bedroom.

'I just need to be careful,' I say. 'You know, with being naughty. I can't get in much more trouble.'

'Good luck with that,' Emma laughs. 'You're the worst girl in Red House.'

I stare at her. 'Very funny.'

But this makes her laugh harder. 'I'm not joking, Bec.'

'Hang on,' I say, reaching out as she starts to walk on. 'You're saying out of everyone in Red House, you think I'm the most badly behaved?'

Emma blinks. 'Well,' she says, 'it's all relative, isn't it?'

I watch her walk down the path and disappear beneath the steps. She must be winding me up. She can't really think that, can she?

~

No one in Yellow House will look at us. The girl beside me still has flour in her dark hair. I search up and down their line for Freya, spotting her near the front. 'Bitches,' someone snarls as they file into the dining hall.

Near the end of breakfast Miss Lacey comes over to our table. I haven't touched my piece of toast. I watch as she leans in, whispering in Briohny's ear, then Portia's. 'Rebecca,' she says when she reaches me, 'Mr Pegg would like to see you in his office after breakfast.'

I expect disappointment, even disgust, when I look up from my lap. Instead Miss Lacey gazes at me with pity, which I think is worse.

Mr Pegg gives me three Queen Rivers; a Queen River is a ten-kilometre run to The Junction and back. A shiver of worry works its way down my spine. I have heard all about these runs. They are worse than Stonely Roads—much worse: the track is rocky, all the way to the creek, and I'll have to go on my own, before dawn, in the dark.

With a fluttering voice I ask about my scholarship. 'Is it all right? Is it safe?'

Mr Pegg stares me down. 'You're skating on thin ice, Rebecca,' he says. 'This is a serious situation. This morning I called your father to speak with him about your behaviour. He is very concerned and has decided to come up for a meeting this week.'

I begin chewing on my fingernails, tearing down at the loose tags of skin. I'd rather one hundred Queen Rivers than face Dad about this.

After school, Libby wanders into the house. She's the daughter of Mr Hillman, the teacher who lives with his family in the brown house down the road. Libby, who is about six or seven, isn't like other children—there is something slow about the way she walks and talks. Her hair is dark, shining auburn when it catches the light, and her enormous blue eyes are always slightly vacant as they roam across your face.

When I first saw Libby I was reminded of the old-fashioned doll I used to have perched on a shelf in my bedroom. That doll frightened me; she always seemed to be watching me when I woke in the morning, her straw bonnet oddly tilted, her small pink lips curled into a snarl.

Libby spots Portia flicking through a magazine and heads straight towards her. A few minutes later Portia has taught her how to stick up her middle finger. Girls gather around the bed to watch.

'There, Libby,' Portia says. 'Now, you do this when you go home and see Daddy. And then you say, *Fuck you*.'

Laughter bristles through the dorm, but it is weighted, expectant. Portia's laugh is unlike anything I've heard—raw and caustic. She reaches out to me, gently pinching the flesh above my elbow. I hate it when she does that.

Libby starts jumping up and down, clapping her tiny hands, a thin stream of dribble running from her mouth. When I glance around I see how the girls are watching me, waiting, and I let out a strained laugh. Portia stops pinching.

I have Solo that night. It's a compulsory night out camping in the bush on your own, and everyone has to do it once during first term. It's a time, the teachers told us, for quiet self-reflection, and to feel totally at ease with the bush. Before going to sleep we're expected to write a letter to ourselves, which at the end of the year will be posted home.

After dinner I'm driven in a Jeep with a few kids from other houses and dropped off at my site, a dry clearing surrounded by tall trees and clusters of prickly bushes.

By the time I set up it is dark. Inside the tent I lie in my sleeping bag with my knees curled to my chin. The tent smells of hiking—a stale stench of wood smoke and dirt and sweaty socks. My guts churn whenever I think of Dad's visit tomorrow.

As a distraction I busy myself with my pack, recalling how Simone said that on her Solo she heard the tinkle of Bobo the Clown. This makes me feel worse. I switch on the torch and poke my head outside. There is nothing out there, of course. Just large stars sparkling in the sky, the drifting scent of eucalyptus.

Back in the tent I pull a beanie hard over my hair and cry for a while. Why do they make us camp on our own like this, barely past the school's boundary? It just seems cruel.

Through my tears I skim the pages of the Solo kit, a booklet of inspirational quotes about living in the outdoors, appreciating nature and having a sense of personal calm and purpose.

After a while I grow tired of crying and begin writing the letter to myself. *Dear Rebecca*, I begin:

> *Well, you are a year older and hopefully wiser after the great Silver Creek year. I hope you also found it the best year of your life.*
>
> *At the moment, I love school and schoolwork, hiking and running. I love the boys and most of the girls. Our House is the best . . .*

When I've finished, I read the letter once over before sealing it back inside the floral envelope. I know I'm not telling the whole truth about everything that's going on up here, but by the end of the year I hope my feelings do reflect these words; that there will be more veracity to them. And perhaps, in the years to come, this is how I will in fact remember everything.

Back in the sleeping bag, I listen for sounds outside, but I can't hear much—only the occasional hoot of a night bird or the rustle of a breeze—and clasping my hands together I snuggle further into the warm bag. I think about the booklet. Most of the quotes are lame, like the one about no bird soaring too high with its own wings, but I liked the one from Walt Whitman, 'Song of the Open Road': *Now I see the secret of the making of the best persons / It is to grow in the open air, and to eat and sleep with the earth.*

Dad sits in the corner of the office, rising only to give me a scrape of a kiss. He's dressed for work in his suit and tie, and I realise that is where he must have come from earlier this morning. He looks exhausted.

Mr Pegg does most of the talking—about Silver Creek and its values. At the window, behind Mr Pegg's head, leaves press against the glass. Dad crosses his legs, his left foot moving up and down in a familiar gesture of irritation. I suppose he doesn't need to hear about standards and expectations—he is a school principal, after all. Suddenly I am ashamed—more ashamed than I've ever been. *Poor Dad*, I think. *This must be so embarrassing.*

When Mr Pegg finally moves on to my misdemeanours and punishments, I clasp my hands together to stop them from shaking: dorm raids, out of bounds, talking after lights-out, a 'general leader of trouble in the house', Stonely Roads and Queen Rivers. He even mentions an essay I wrote in English, comparing Silver Creek to *Animal Farm*—'I mean, really?' he scoffs.

Eventually Dad clears his throat and asks about my scholarship. 'Does Rebecca's behaviour put the arrangement in jeopardy?'

Mr Pegg takes a while to answer, but then with a sigh says it is fine—for now. But my behaviour must improve. 'You're running out of chances,' he tells me.

Afterwards, I walk with Dad to the car park. It is a warm afternoon, the big eucalypts rustling like maracas.

Dad leans against the bonnet of the Pajero, rubbing at his eyes. 'I just don't understand all this, Rebecca,' he says, glancing at me from beneath his bushy eyebrows. 'You've never been in this kind of trouble before.'

'I'm sorry,' I mumble.

He touches the tip of his shoe to the front wheel. 'Is there anything you need to tell me? About the house, or any of the girls?'

'No,' I say. 'It's all fine.'

He looks away, over the line of grey-green trees. He takes a deep breath, exhales loudly. 'We're worried about you. Your mother and I. You're so far away. We just don't understand why you're behaving like this . . .'

'I'm fine, Dad,' I say. 'Really. It isn't going to happen again.'

He watches me, squinting. Except for the occasional burst of anger, my dad never shows a lot of emotion. Now he looks sad.

'I won't be naughty anymore,' I say, firmer this time. 'I'll be good, I promise.'

He nods, his eyes sliding to the ground. He doesn't believe me.

I watch the car crawl down the road, growing small and shiny like a beetle until it disappears near the piggery, and then I squat in the gutter. I'm so tired—I could lie down on the scratchy grass and sleep for hours. But we're leaving on a hike this afternoon, camping tonight on the edge of Mount Stonely. I can't think of anything worse.

I put my head between my knees. A few flies buzz around, and I play with the soft hair on my shins. How like my parents it is for Dad to make the trip up here, to be the disciplinarian. That's how it has always been in my family. Mum is the one who lets you get away with things; she is softer, more malleable.

But I wish it had been Mum to come up here to find out what was going on. That she had asked me *something* about how I was feeling. I picture her at home, sitting in the back room, a cup of tea on the table, sunlight streaming through the French windows. I've seen her like that a thousand times, but right now I can't make out her face.

I feel out of sorts after Dad's visit. I know I promised him I'd be good, but I don't feel like being good. I become irritable around the house, snapping at anyone who gets on my nerves.

Sometimes I lie in bed at night and want to break things. Pieces of furniture, mainly, but sometimes I also think about hurting people—the girls. Sometimes I picture myself hitting them in the face: Briohny usually. These thoughts frighten me, but probably not as much as they should. I don't know where they come from or how to stop them.

I'm not the only one in the house acting different. Lou has grown quiet and withdrawn. She doesn't laugh as much as she used to, and whenever she smiles there is something pained about it. I don't know why her parents sent her to Silver Creek when she loves the farm so much. I know her dad was a student at the school, and her grandfather before him. Maybe these traditions are more important.

One night Lou and Sarah come back from music practice drunk. They'd snuck into the vestry and skolled the Communion wine. 'All of it!' Sarah screeched.

Miss McKinney is on duty tonight; she's due to drop in any minute. Simone and I haul Lou to the bathroom to sober her up, making her brush her teeth and then pushing her into the shower.

But Sarah won't be drawn. Instead she runs up and down the dorm, grabbing any loose items from beds and tossing them on the floor.

'Is she crazy?' Portia breathes. 'McKinney is coming up the road.'

Sarah balances on a metal bed end, still laughing hard. But her eyes seem determined to me, controlled. Perhaps she wants to get caught.

Miss McKinney walks in just as Sarah crashes to the floor. Red-faced and sweating, she gazes up at the assistant and lets out a giant burp.

'Oh, Jesus,' Miss McKinney says, and to my surprise she laughs.

After Miss McKinney takes Sarah away, Miss Lacey arrives. She makes us line up so she can smell our breath. My heart races when she reaches Lou, but she takes a sniff, nods, and moves on to the next girl. After searching the house for contraband, Miss Lacey seems satisfied there is nothing to be found. Sarah, she tells us, has been suspended for a week. Tomorrow she will be driven down to Melbourne to stay with her guardians.

A few nights later, Portia and Briohny do another Bell Run. They've been bragging about it all week. As they get ready, they make a big deal about who they're going to ask to join them. 'Bec?' Briohny scoffs when my name is mentioned. 'Not that *suck*.' I hear Portia snort.

It seems like they've been gone for hours before the bell gongs across the school, and moments later they come galloping back through the dorm.

I check my watch. It's 3.12 am. I feel hysteria start to build in my chest, almost vibrating—I desperately need to sleep.

'Can you be quiet?' I shout.

'Fuck off.' Briohny laughs and throws something hard at my bed. 'You keep us awake all the time.'

'I don't care. Just shut up, will you?'

But they don't listen. They chatter for hours, laughing off other complaints. I don't say another thing to Briohny—I don't trust what might come out of my mouth, what I might do. My dislike of her has transformed into something keener, sharper. I'm afraid of it.

~

There is another long run that afternoon. This one takes us past the dam and over the hills to the west of the campus, along a narrow path dipping down by the creek.

I keep thinking the runs will get easier as we get fitter, but they never do—each one is more excruciating than the last. At the finish line I stare down at my place card, blood rushing to my head. I've ranked somewhere in the middle of the field of girls. Average.

I wander over to the tree on the small lawn, lingering for a moment to catch my breath. I want to go back to the house, and when no one is looking I creep around the library and up the steps. In an alcove I glimpse Portia in a circle of boys, Rollo Walker beside her. He's wearing a Bintang T-shirt and red footy shorts. Even from here I can see the hair at his nape is wet with sweat.

I wave, hoping Portia might invite me over so I'll have the chance to talk to Rollo. But as her eyes meet mine her face changes, hardening. I've seen this look a dozen times, and the hair on my arms tingles. She says something quietly to Rollo, making him laugh, before she turns away.

~

That night I scuttle down the stairs, late for dinner. The bell must have been rung because lines are already forming. I don't want the teachers to see me coming in late, so when Miss Lacey's back is turned I make a beeline for the spot at the front. But I didn't see Briohny, and as I slip my way in she lunges at me, hissing, 'Go to the back of the line!'

I stand my ground. She shoves me again, right on my spine. Before I know what I'm doing I've grabbed her around the collar, my vision narrowing, only aware of my white knuckles, my voice, which has gone strangely hollow and tinny inside my head, and the words working their way from my gritted teeth are foul, awful words that I can never take back. I hoist her higher. *Now who's smirking, you cunt.* I want to hit her, really smash her face in. That'll show her that she can't push me around. That will show her that I am strong, someone to be feared. But Briohny isn't fighting back, she's just staring at me, her head jolting around like a ragdoll.

Miss Lacey comes out of nowhere and tears me away. 'What the hell are you *doing*?'

I stagger from the line, woozy. *What is wrong with me?* Miss Lacey has her hands on her hips, waiting for my answer. But no words come.

Briohny tugs at her collar. 'She pushed in. Then started *fighting* me!'

Now Miss Lacey grabs my arm, twisting it. I can see the red threads in her eyes, smell the beer on her breath. 'You're this close, Rebecca. *This* close . . .' She holds up two fingers like pincers. 'And despite what you think, you don't get special treatment around here. So get to the back of the bloody line.'

I scuff my way to the rear of the amphitheatre. Kendall is standing there, but she doesn't turn around. Is she scared of me too? The thought is awful, and my lip begins to quiver.

Now why did you do that?

~

There is a film screening after dinner: *The Princess Bride* with Cary Elwes. All the girls think he is hot. But I go back to the house. I want some time on my own, to walk around the dorm with no one looking, to think about things I'm never able to up here—like stories and characters and dialogue I've made up in my head. I want to talk to myself.

But I find Kendall, lying on her bed, reading a book. She raises a hand to me, a small nod of a greeting. I smile tightly.

We sit in companionable silence. This isn't so bad. I make a cup of Milo and take it to the deck, where I watch the sunset until mosquitoes come out and start to bite around my ankles.

Back inside, Kendall has swapped her book for sewing. I lean out my window, tracing my finger along the dusty sill, breathing in the night air. It is the only thing I'll miss during the holidays—the air. Tonight it smells slightly damp, with the faintest hint of wood smoke swept up from somewhere down the hill.

I run a shower and sing under the hot water, old tunes from *The Phantom of the Opera*, which I used to listen to on my Walkman, always crying at the part where the phantom loses Christine. I scrub at my arms. They've grown so brown—my legs, too, slim and sturdy as poles. I watch the shampoo suds stream over my breasts and down my body, circling the plughole before disappearing. I turn off the taps and wring out my hair. Have I changed? I wonder, as I pad across the tiles to the bench. When I look into the mirror, it does seem like a stranger is staring back.

It is night. Blue shadows move around Yellow House, shifting and morphing near the basketball ring, the house beyond it, illuminated by a single square-shaped light. I stare at the patch of road that veers off to make a path. The breeze picks up for a moment before dropping away with a sigh. And then, from the shadows, emerges a dark mass. Arms and legs and hiking boots. They move with such silent stealth they could be almost floating along the road. I can't see faces, just the outline of their movement. But when the moon drifts out from behind a cloud, bathing the road in an urgent sort of light, I see how they're all gazing up towards Red House.

'They're coming back,' I murmur. I turn to Kendall, and she puts her sewing aside, eyes on me. They never waver.

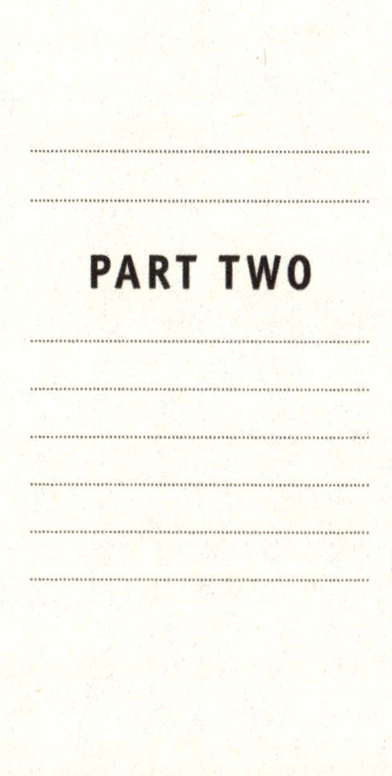

PART TWO

8

I start up the engine and drive on, over the cattle grid and up the first incline. My hands are sweaty on the wheel. Rain has begun to fleck the windscreen and the wind howls at the windows.

When I come to the closed gate I almost cry out with relief. I won't be able to go in after all. But it isn't locked—nothing at Silver Creek is ever locked. I'd forgotten this rule: that you are encouraged to trust those you live with.

The road dips and curves, and some blue sky creeps out from behind the clouds. The vineyard has grown, the vines heartier, spreading across the length of the paddock. Everything else seems unchanged.

I pass the sheds, the vegetable garden, and the pen where the pigs were kept. I can't see any today. Further along is the hayshed. It looks creepy, almost derelict, with cobwebs billowing in the breeze.

Just before the library I pull over beside a rash of wattle on the yellow lawn. I probably shouldn't take the car all the way up to Red House. I check the rear-view mirror, then the other windows. I chew on my fingernails, furtive. No one is around. It is school holidays—the students are away, off-campus. But I still can't shake the feeling that I'm sneaking around.

I rest my hands on the steering wheel, the steady pulse of the engine throbbing through my fingertips. I hadn't expected these nerves. I'd mulled over the idea to visit Silver Creek for ages, always feeling rather clinical about it. *It's only a school*, I'd told myself. *You're only going to remind yourself of the landscape and smells and the 'feel' of the place.* But now that I'm here, hunched over in the car, it does seem *wrong*. What if I run into someone? I can't tell them what I'm writing about: the school is so private. They would take it the wrong way.

I've only come back once to Silver Creek since I left, when my parents and I dropped Archie off for his year away. I was only a couple of years out of school myself, but still a teenager, still naïve. Still with the arrogant swagger of a graduate student; an Old Girl. How different that feeling is now, ten years later. Shouldn't I have grown easier in my own skin?

I climb out of the car, grabbing my scarf, and head towards the chapel. On the way I pass the block of classrooms, with its low verandah extending from one side to the other keeping the doors and windows in perpetual gloom. Somewhere in there is Mr Pegg's old office. He's not the headmaster anymore, but I still imagine him sitting inside, behind that big wooden desk. Thinking of Mr Pegg sends panic rising in my chest. Why does being back here make me feel so *guilty*?

Tiny gumnuts fleck the path. The chapel looms ahead, dwarfing everything. I expect it to be locked, but the doors are pitched open in the gravel. When I take off my sunglasses, everything swims for a minute. Ahead, between me and the altar, are pews, a dozen rows on either side of the aisle, while on my left is the vestry.

Each week, in that cramped, dusty room, I would take viola lessons with Miss Heart, a silver-haired woman with nicotine-stained teeth. The morning light used to flare against the window, illuminating—alarmingly—the whiskers on Miss Heart's chin.

I take a seat in the back pew. I've rarely been inside a church since school. I run my finger over hymnbooks, think about picking one up. I close my eyes, dwelling on the quiet. These days I don't enjoy a lot of silence—time is always filled with sound or movement or thinking, my mind rarely still, always flitting, like a kaleidoscope. That's what I'd liked about chapel—the moments of quiet reflection—and, shuffling my boots across the smooth bluestone, I suddenly think of Lara.

I haven't thought about Lara in a long time. Years, in fact. We knew each other in primary school. Lara lived with her mum in an enormous house overlooking the beach, with a pool at the back and an air-hockey table in a room they called the den. She had a black poodle called Soda who used to jump up and scrabble painfully at my legs every time I went to her house.

Lara had the best clothes of any kid in my class—OshKosh T-shirts and new Reebok Pumps every six months. (She used to give me her hand-me-downs, which I would wear until the soles fell away.) She even had a television in her room with a Nintendo.

Her dad didn't live with Lara. He had remarried another, younger woman, and they lived in a house in the city. Sometimes Lara and I stayed over at her dad's house. He'd often go out for the evening, his wife wearing a cocktail dress, and when they were gone Lara would bring out the *Nightmare on Elm Street* or

Pet Sematary videos. At home I wasn't allowed to watch anything with more than a PG rating, and these films gave me nightmares. While Lara snored softly beside me, I'd lie awake for hours listening to the noise of traffic, my eyes fixed on the weird glow of the fish tank, full of guppies and pink and blue coral, in the corner of the room.

I was so proud to be Lara's best friend. She was smart and interesting, and everyone at school liked her.

Like most girls that age, our friendship was intense, passionate even. We spent so much time together: every day at school and several afternoons a week at one another's homes, and almost every weekend we organised a sleepover. She was the first person outside my family that I truly loved.

I had always been an obedient child. I was studious and well behaved in class, eager to please my teachers and do well on tests and assignments. I didn't have a huge number of friends, but I was often invited over to play and attend birthday parties. And I also knew my own mind from an early age, knew that I wanted to do well for myself.

But with Lara that independence seemed to disappear. I would do anything she asked of me, no matter if it got me in trouble. If she wanted me to call another girl names, I'd do it. If she wanted me to steal from the milk bar, I'd do it. I was never afraid of the consequences. My only fear was of losing her.

Lara didn't like my brother. She said he was annoying. It was odd, really: she and Archie looked alike, both with red hair, freckles and creamy skin. They could have been siblings. But Lara was an only child: she never knew what it was to share someone.

Whenever Lara came over to the house Archie wanted to play with us. He liked Lara; he liked everyone. He was only four or five, but we never let him join in. 'Tell him to go *away*,' Lara would whisper in my ear, her breath warm against my cheek. 'Tell him to *get lost*.'

I'd always hesitate, looking from my brother to her. 'Do it,' she said, pinching my arm, and I stood up and pushed Archie so hard he toppled over. 'Piss off, freckle-face fart machine,' I growled.

The words were salty, almost acidic, as they passed through my lips. Instantly I wished I could take them back. I loved my brother. He was my friend; we played together, had our own secrets from Mum and Dad. Tears welled in Archie's eyes, his cheeks mottling, and after he'd run wailing from the room Lara sat back, grinning.

Later Mum drew me aside to ask, incredulously, why I couldn't be *nice* to him? I could feel the disappointment in her uncertain grip around my wrist, and guilt dropped through me like a shaft.

I stand up, lurching along the pews. It's so dark in the chapel I can barely see my own feet. It's awful to remember how cruel I'd been to my brother, all for Lara.

In the end our friendship soured. Maybe it would have anyway, but at the time I blamed it on the arrival of a new girl to our grade.

Taylor was blonde and boyish, with an undercut and a stud at the top of her ear. Lara took an immediate interest in her. From day one she was always trying to catch Taylor's eye, or say something witty to get her attention. Before I knew it Lara was saving Taylor a seat on the bench in the playground, and sitting next to her in class. At lunchtime they stalked off to the canteen together, leaving me to chew morosely at my Vegemite sandwiches until they returned with steaming meat pies and cartons of Big M.

I tried to brush it off. I didn't like Taylor—she was loud and brutish and not very smart; she couldn't even do her twelve times tables. Lara would grow sick of her and come back to me. I just had to wait it out.

But then one day Lara didn't ask me to join them in the playground and I felt the first prickle of fear. Then the invitations to her house after school stopped. I sat alone in class, sniggers cast my way from their desk, until one morning I turned around and told Taylor it wasn't my fault she was illiterate. She launched herself across the desk, grabbing my fingers and bending them back until I begged for mercy. The teacher made us both sit in the corner until the bell rang.

All this I could weather because I still held out hope that my friendship with Lara might be restored. That she would recognise my unique position in her affections. But weeks grew into months and still we weren't reconciled.

At home I grew sullen. I never told my parents what happened, but they must have known. Each night I'd lie awake for hours, wretchedly tired, screeching that I couldn't sleep. For close to a year I slept barely four hours a night.

The term finally ended and summer holidays began. When I returned to school after the long break I was in a new grade, without Lara. I hardly saw her around the playground, though when I did I always felt my breath catch. After all that had happened, I still wanted, so desperately, for her to like me again. For her to forgive me for whatever I had done.

I stumble out the chapel door. My eyes get starry, readjusting from the dark. I stand with a hand against the stone wall, holding myself up. I am shaking, almost in tears. 'Sometimes,' my mother once said to me, 'you have to let go of the things that hurt you most. You just have to go . . . poof.' And she'd opened her hands, palms wide, facing the sky.

After all these years, I don't know if I'd even recognise Lara if I saw her in the street. But the memory of her and the memory of me—so acquiescent, so weak—is fresh like an open-cut wound.

~

I walk on, along the orange road dimpled like a corn chip. I pass Miss Lacey's old house tucked away on the slope, a cluster of trees out the front, and then Mr Hillman's on the embankment. Two pairs of boots, one big, one small, rest neatly on the front step. I wonder if Mr Hillman and Libby still live there. Which is silly, really. Almost all the teachers from my time have moved on.

Red House looks much the same, except for tufts of grass and a few trees out the front. Curtains hang in the windows. The rocks out the front, once bald and conspicuous, have taken on a sculpted, elegant quality. The place is nearly pretty.

I glance around, furtive again. I want to laugh. I'm a grown woman cowering like a teenager. *You didn't have to come here*, I remind myself. *No one made you.* That it was my choice now seems ludicrous as I linger near a pile of stones in the shape of a cairn, afraid to move.

Clutching my notebook, I walk up the clay path. The deck is empty except for the metal washing crate near the steps, lined with a giant calico. The drying room door is shut. The wind stirs up a low moan through the trees. I move towards the banister, peering over the empty road. There is no one around, no one following me.

I turn back and put my nose to the window. I can make out the desks, the fireplace and, only just, the first bed through the doorway to the dorm. Can almost smell it, the house. The wood sanding, the dust, the girls—the moisturiser, shampoo, sweet sweat. I can smell it all, and my heart starts to beat hard as I open the front door and step inside.

9

It's strange to be home for the holidays, sleeping in my own bed. Only I won't be sleeping in it for long. Nan is coming to stay. She has been in hospital again, and now Mum is looking after her until arrangements can be made. I don't know what these arrangements are. All I know is one evening Nan climbed out of her hospital bed and fell over.

'She had a stroke,' Dad explains on the drive back from the bus depot. 'A small one, but still serious enough.' He tugs at his tie, then moves his hand to my shoulder. 'She's okay, but she's not quite herself.'

We are driving across the West Gate Bridge, over the murky mouth of the Yarra River and all those petrol silos. My eyes drift towards the horizon and the sea, unbroken but for the power station's eerie cooling tower, shaped like a cigarette with red bands for a glowing tip. The news seems unreal to me. Nan is tough and wiry, with a cheeky smile. She spends all day outside in her enormous orchid garden, her ancient moggy, Pushka, basking on the deck. She may be old but she still dresses neatly and cooks for herself (lamb chops with steamed vegetables is her speciality). How can *she* need looking after? She has always been the one to look after Archie and me. It must be a mistake. Dad must have heard the story from Mum and unknowingly exaggerated it, like a Chinese whisper.

But a few days later Nan comes through the front door, leaning on a stick. She drifts along the hallway, dabbing at the edges of picture frames, her wispy hair spilling from a pin. Her face is covered in maroon bruises.

We all gather in the kitchen. Mum makes cups of tea that no one drinks. I watch Nan sitting with her hands in her lap. She doesn't speak, except to smile at me and call me Margot, which is my mother's name.

I don't want to see her like this, strange and ghostly-looking and muddled. I run away to my room, but Mum comes after me.

'I'm going to set Nan up in here,' she says. 'I'll make you up a bed in the front room instead.'

'The front room?' I say. 'On the camping bed? Oh, this is great. Just *great*! I get to spend *my* holidays on the *camping bed*. Thanks very much.'

Mum sighs. Framed in the doorway, a damp dishcloth slung over her shoulder, I can see how exhausted she is, sad lines etched around her mouth, and I wish I hadn't said anything.

After she's gone I sit at my doll's house in front of the hearth. It was a present from Nan for my fifth birthday. I pick up the figurines. Over the years I have disfigured them horribly and now the family of a father, mother, son and daughter are amputees, red-pen blood splattered across their faces and torsos, their miniature clothing ripped to shreds.

I turn the daughter over in my palm. I've never liked her, or her short blonde hair and white tunic, and I twist her rubbery arm until it almost breaks.

~

I wake up several times in the night. Boxes and furniture that doesn't fit in other rooms in the house surround the camping bed. It's so dark in here—the heavy curtain blocks out all the light. I sit up, straining to hear something, the bedsprings heaving beneath me. But there's only silence.

The next day my old friend Tash visits. We play a bit of Nintendo then take our tennis racquets down to the concrete courts at the local high school. I pretend I'm Anna Kournikova and Tash is Martina Hingis. Tash always beats me.

Some days we spend the whole afternoon searching for pictures of Prince William on the internet. Those we like are printed off on Dad's colour printer. My favourites are from Princess Diana's funeral. We stick them in my diary and Tash writes: *Yummy! What a babe!* Then she glues in her own picture of Jonathan Taylor Thomas, enclosing it in a lavish heart.

Tash stays over one night, sleeping on a mattress beside my camping bed. We don't talk about Silver Creek. We don't talk much at all. Usually I don't mind. But tonight I'd like to tell her about Red House, about Portia and Kendall and all the others. I'd like to ask who she spends time with while I'm away, and whether she likes any boys. Tash and I have known each other for years and years and in some ways our friendship hasn't changed, nearly every emotion and feeling left unsaid, as it was when we were six years old.

My family don't ask me much about the term away either. My parents, I'm discovering, always talk around Silver Creek. They ask constantly if I've enough tuck or if I'll be warm enough next term, but not about my friendships, or whether I've missed home. Dad's visit is never mentioned, nor the reason for it.

One evening, however, Archie teases me about one of Mr Pegg's letters. 'Mum and Dad are always talking about you,' he says, laughing. 'About how bad you are, and how they wish you'd never gone to Silver Creek. "What is she doing?" Mum always says. "What is she *thinking*?"'

'Really?' I look over at Mum tipping a packet of frozen peas into a pot. 'Well, it's all sorted now.'

Archie has already wandered off, the television beckoning. Mum stays at the stovetop, staring at the flame. Her shoulders are stooped, the slightly rounded top of her back flushed red. When she glances at me her eyes are glinting, the same as when she watches Nan floating around the backyard. As if she'd lost something.

~

There is no moon tonight, and the air is colder than it's been all year. My breath comes out as fog. The bus from Melbourne was late getting in. On the way up Simone and I chatted giddily about the holidays, but now we drag our bags up the hill towards the house in silence. I wonder if she is as apprehensive as I am.

I sense it the moment I walk into the dorm. Something has changed. Not in the look of the place—my bed is still pushed against the wall, covered in the faded crescent-moon doona cover—but in the air, like an electrical storm.

Girls are gathered on Sarah's bed in the corner. Portia is in the middle, and they laugh as she points to something in a magazine.

After I've put down my bags, I wander towards them. Sarah is the only one to look up and she smiles thinly. Her acne has cleared over the holidays.

'Hi guys,' I say. 'What are you reading?'

'Just a magazine.' Sarah yawns.

'Which one?'

Portia glares. 'Just a magazine.' This makes Sarah laugh, a braying sound, and I hear *suck* muttered from somewhere. I return to my bed, my stomach congealed. Since when have they been so chummy?

Later, as I brush my teeth, I catch Ronnie admiring her new haircut in the mirror. 'Looks nice,' I say shyly, wiping my chin with my T-shirt.

Ronnie smiles, preening in the glass. 'I like to have something different now and again,' she says. Leaning against my shoulder, she gazes mildly at my reflection—our reflection, really. I don't know what to say, but I like the feel of her arm against me. Ronnie doesn't seem to notice; now she's baring her teeth, picking at them with floss.

~

My bed area is failed during the first house inspection back. I hadn't made my bed properly and my side table was cluttered with mugs and books and chocolate wrappers. Making a note on her clipboard, Miss Lacey promises to fail the entire house if I don't have it tidy tomorrow.

'Good one, Rebecca,' Briohny mutters on her way to the study.

Walking back from class at recess, I glimpse something in the dirt outside my window. Nearer, I realise it's my doona, and poking beneath it my mattress along with everything from my bedside table. It's all filthy.

Briohny appears at the windowsill. 'Next time make sure it's tidy, you dickhead,' she says.

Portia leans out further and lets a string of saliva drop near my feet. 'Next time,' she says, 'we'll throw *you* out the window.'

They laugh, ducking back inside. I reach down and pick up

one of my trolls, shaking dust from its pink hair. Why are they picking on me?

~

'Have you noticed anything weird since we got back?'

It's morning. I've stopped on the path beneath the chapel so Emma can tie her shoelaces. She always leaves the house half dressed; I feel like this is how we conduct all our conversations—with her straining to adjust some item of clothing.

'What do you mean?'

'Portia.' I sigh. 'She's being weird around me, like she hates me or something.'

Emma zips up her polar fleece. 'Yeah,' she says. 'I've noticed.'

I raise my eyes to the enormous cross. Birdshit stains the tip like dripping wax. 'But what have I done wrong?'

'You haven't *done* anything,' Emma says. 'That's just how Portia is. She's got her favourites and then she moves on to someone new. Don't worry about it.'

I reach out to help her up. If only it were that easy. If only I was more like Emma, untouched by what others think or say. She never needs anyone's approval. I'm not like that—I will worry until I've got to the bottom of it, even if I know I won't like what I find. I still don't know how to change that about myself.

~

Autumn has bleached everything grey. Sunlight, when it does appear, merely splinters across the sky. Even the smells around the campus are tarnished. And it rains now, steady rain falling in large, icy drops.

One afternoon Ronnie gets a letter from home. After she's read it, she flings herself across her bed, wailing, and her contortions of grief make me want to fall on the ground and weep too.

'Her dog died,' I hear someone whisper.

When Ronnie finally drags herself up, she takes a few deep breaths and wipes her eyes, before folding the letter over and tucking it inside her top drawer. There is something defiant in her face, something grainy and hard.

Everyone is miserable during the first weeks back at school. There is more crying, especially at night, before bed. Letters come from home that seem to set one girl off at a time, until half the house is in tears, including me.

'What's the matter?' Emma asks when she finds me sobbing at the end of the bed.

'I don't know,' I say, letting out a strangled laugh. 'I'm just sad.'

It must be the cold depleting our spirits. Last term it was fine not having any heating because the house still stayed warm into the night. But now it's cold all the time. The study is the worst: even with the fire roaring, a draught seems to stalk along the floor and work its way into my clothes.

One night there's a particularly nasty draught in the study. When Simone and I go to inspect its source, we find one of the dorm's back windows still open. Too high to reach, we take my desk chair down the other end of the aisle. Simone almost has the pane shut when Miss McKinney walks in.

'What are you doing?'

I smile at Simone. *Der, what does it look like?*

'It's freezing in the study, so we're just closing this window.'

Miss McKinney isn't listening. 'You should have asked my permission to leave your desks,' she says. 'Get down from there.'

Simone doesn't move. 'I'm almost done.'

I watch Miss McKinney reach out and begin to shake the chair. Simone teeters, and for a moment I think she'll fall. Alarm flashes in her dark eyes, swiftly followed by another, steelier look.

'I said get down!'

I've always liked Miss McKinney. She isn't hard like some teachers. Most mornings at chapel she sings in a faltering soprano. 'Jerusalem' is her favourite. Tonight her fringe is greasy, her glasses smudged with fingerprints. There are fresh lines around her eyes—stress lines, probably. It would be so easy to make fun of her; she can't know how hard we try not to—if she did, she wouldn't be acting like this.

Now Miss McKinney turns to me. 'You know,' she says, 'the problem with you girls is you think you can do whatever you want.'

Simone and I are marched down the hill to the science labs. Miss McKinney puts us in separate rooms, locking us inside. It's even colder and draughtier in here than it was in the house.

I call out to Simone, but when I don't get a reply I sit at a desk, shivering under the throbbing lights. Every now and then I'm startled by sounds outside, but eventually I rest my head on the desk and close my eyes.

It seems like hours before Miss McKinney returns. When she finally unlocks the door, she stands on the landing and beckons me, smacking her hands against her thighs, like she would to a dog. 'So,' she says, escorting Simone and me back to the house, 'have you learnt your lesson?' When we don't reply she begins to whistle.

In the dorm everyone is tucked up in bed, the lights already out. We've missed weekly supper, which I had been looking forward to all evening. While Simone and I get changed in the tog room, Portia barks for us to hurry up. 'You're keeping us awake!'

By the time I'm warm under the covers I need to get up for the toilet. As I creep along the aisle I hear muffled crying. It's coming from Simone's bed. I stop, my arms and legs bristling in the cold. I know I should go to her, see if she is all right, but I can feel Portia's eyes locked on me from the pocket of darkness around her bed, so I walk past without even pausing.

10

~

It's dark when my alarm goes off for slush. It's only my second morning on duty, but it still takes every ounce of willpower to throw back the covers. Huddled at the end of the bed, I pull on a pair of ratty jeans, a flannel shirt that belonged to Dad and a woollen jumper, grabbing my Blundstones from my locker in the tog room.

Behind the chapel a hazy sun starts to rise, dragging up a few clouds. I lurch down the path, steam shooting from my mouth. At the steps I always stop to gaze out across the campus. I don't know why I do this—everything has been dulled by the wintery sky, like silver with the shine worn off. I haven't seen blue in weeks, while the rain now falls on the house's tin roof with the persistence of a metronome.

In the kitchen Monsieur Gerrard, our chef, is hunched over a stainless-steel bench. The room is filled with the heady stench of breakfast: enormous vats of porridge and baked beans bubble on the stove, bacon sizzles and cracks on the grill. Further along is the industrial toaster, which runs like a conveyer belt with row after row of sliced bread.

'Hi, Monsieur Gerrard,' I call.

He spins around. He's brandishing a meat cleaver, and his white apron is spattered with blood. '*Bonjour*, Rebecca!' He holds up a skinless creature by the feet. '*Lapin*,' he says with a grin. 'Rabbit.'

I prepare my serving trolley, stacking the trays with bowls and plates still warm from the wash; aluminium containers of food at the top. Once the other slushies have done the same, we all sit down to our own breakfast.

Across the table is Max, from Blue House. He has dark hair and dark eyes—he's Jewish, I've heard. I've never met a Jewish person before and I turn red any time he looks at me. I suppose I have a crush on him, and later that night I write in my diary, *I love Max*. It's the first time I've written about a boy, but I wouldn't tell anyone that. Simone's diary is practically blacked out with all her declarations of love, a new name just about every day. But as I stare at those three words, imprisoned in a garish red heart, it seems more and more like an illusion, and my eyes start to swim, until the letters have broken up and floated away.

~

The early mornings begin to take their toll. Large, angry bruises appear beneath my eyes, while my skin has a yellowish tinge to it. I develop a cough that brings up phlegm laced with blood. In class I hardly say a word, sitting in the back row, wishing I could put my head down on the laminate desk and sleep for weeks. Except that I'm chilled to my bones—the classrooms aren't heated, either. Only in science is anyone animated, jostling around the Bunsen burners like they're open fireplaces.

I'm also not sleeping well. No matter how exhausted I am, as soon as my head hits the pillow I'm wide awake, my mind racing. Mostly I think about Portia—how I might try to talk to her in the morning, what I might say to make her laugh. During the day I feel constantly on edge, paranoid about how to act around her and Ronnie and Briohny, who always seems to be waiting to catch me out in some blunder.

But it's the cold that keeps me awake most. When the sun drops behind the hill the temperature in the dorm plummets. Some girls have hot-water bottles, which they keep at the end of the bed for their feet. I've written to Mum, asking her to send me one. I go to bed wearing two pairs of socks, a jumper, a beanie and sometimes gloves. Like rot, the cold seems to work its way into my bed, seeping up through the floor and into the mattress. Most nights it feels like I'm lying on a slab of ice, my doona a thin sheet of pastry.

'You don't look so hot,' says Simone one morning on the way to class. 'Are you feeling okay?'

'I'm fine,' I snap. Simone is always smooth-skinned; I don't think I've ever seen her with bags under her eyes.

'Sorry.' She frowns. 'Just asking.'

Watching her trudge off, I want to cry. I wish I could forget about Portia and Briohny and Ronnie, and be happy with the friends I have. Why do I need more?

~

My Outdoor Education teacher, a young man with a big nose and ruddy cheeks, talks a lot about resilience. You need it, he says, for hiking, running, schoolwork. 'You need it for life *itself*,' he says theatrically. But he never says you need resilience for the house, to survive a year with fifteen other girls.

Portia's new favourite is Sarah. They do everything together now—sit with each other at meals, whisper across the study during prep, escape to the bush out the back of the house to smoke.

Whenever I think about them, I feel a bit sick. I don't understand what went wrong. Why doesn't she like me anymore? *How am I different this term from last?* I want to shout at her.

I get it into my head that there's been some kind of misunderstanding. That if I can just talk to Portia about everything, make her understand how much I value our friendship, how important it is to me and how loyal I am to her, things will change. But it's hard to get any time with her around the house. So I start waiting for her after breakfast, jogging to match her pace back up the hill. I offer her lollies from my tuck box when I offer to no one else, not even Emma. I even ask if she'd like me to make her hot chocolate in the evenings.

I shudder at the humiliation of it. I know how it must look. And I can see how the other girls watch on with surprise, knowing their surprise will soon transform into disgust and disrespect. But I can't help myself. I have to be her friend again; I need to know that she cares about me, that I didn't dream the last term.

One night, when I'm brushing my teeth, Ronnie draws me aside. 'Maybe just leave it,' she says, 'around Portia and stuff? Try not to be so . . . I don't know . . . desperate. Yeah, Bec?' Her eyes are gentle, but I recoil as if she'd hit me.

I run sobbing from the bathroom and hide outside behind the woodpile. A few minutes pass before Emma wades into the cold. 'Come on, Bec,' she calls. 'It's time to stop caring so much about Portia.'

'It's fine for you,' I shout back. 'She likes you.'

'But you know she'll soon start hating on someone else,' Emma reasons, wiping her nose on her sleeve. Out here, on the path outside the boiler room, her ragged breath comes out in white clouds. She always breathes like that—loudly, snottily—and it should drive me mad.

'What?' she now says, because I am grinning as I step out from behind the woodpile. I can't help it. I can't believe how easily—how wilfully—I forget how much Emma cares for me. Because I love her back, I really do, like I would love a sister if I had one.

~

Miss Lacey hosts afternoon tea. She offers us scones and cups of coffee, and chocolate bunnies and eggs left over from Easter. Her house is small and brown, same as Red House, with a cramped living area and an electric heater and a television in the corner. But it is cosy, like a proper home, with loads of books lining the shelves.

Miss Lacey pulls out a copy of *The Grapes of Wrath* and hands it to me. 'This is Steinbeck's best,' she says. 'Have a read of it after you've finished *Of Mice and Men* and tell me what you think.' She smiles, and gives my shoulder a squeeze on the way past.

Books are about the only thing Miss Lacey and I talk about with any degree of warmth. She knows so much about literature, and I like these brief moments, when all the old animosity is forgotten and she looks at me like she's interested in what I have to say.

It is kind of Miss Lacey to go to this trouble, I think as she hands around more eggs. Especially after we've been so horrible. I peel off the foil and pop the chocolate into my mouth. Maybe things will be different from now on. Maybe we'll all start to like her again.

We wander back to the house as a group. Everyone is chatty from all the sugar, and from being unexpectedly spoilt. I hang towards the back, reaching over to pick up stones and dropping them back on the ground. Portia walks a few paces ahead of me, but as we near Mr Hillman's house she stops.

'Sorry,' I say after bumping into her.

I feel breath on my neck, can even smell it, sour from the tea, and I turn around. It's Sarah. The whiteheads on her cheeks have returned in an angry rash. She is looking past me, to Portia. Suddenly both girls grab me around the waist.

'Hold her,' Portia says.

As Sarah pins back my arms, Portia begins fumbling with my jeans. I'm too stunned to move. Portia can't get the zip, but my jeans are baggy so she pulls them down over my bum. I watch them reach for my underwear, gathering up the elastic band at the front and back.

'Ready?' Portia says. A vein bulges weirdly at her throat.

They hoist me up by my underwear, lifting me clean off the ground. The pain is awful, burning between my legs. I start thrashing, arms and legs flying about, and I manage to kick Portia in the shin. They drop me.

'You fucking bitches,' I shriek. 'What is *wrong* with you?'

I can hardly see through the tears. Cowering, the cold breeze blows against my bare skin. They've almost torn my underwear in half.

Portia and Sarah glance at each other and laugh, high-fiving. I can just make out the rest of the girls walking further up the road. No one has even noticed what just happened.

In the shower that night I wash my bottom and between my legs, alarmed when the flannel comes away stained with blood. I cry under the hot water, feeling ashamed and dirty. Afterwards, I get dressed in the locked toilet cubicle.

I'm about to climb into bed when I sense someone behind me. Before I can move, icy fingers are at the band of my pyjamas, followed by the nip of the elastic against my waist. I spin around to see Portia stalking back down the aisle.

'Snap,' she says.

11

~

I expect it to be cold inside the house, but the sun blazes through the windows, heating up the study like a conservatory. The smell is familiar, almost cloying: faintly smoky, but also waxy. There are logs in the bin beside the fireplace, and newspapers in a neat stack. The desks are set out just as I remember them, like they've never been moved.

In the dorm I make my way down the aisle, touching the bed ends gingerly. The floorboards creak beneath my feet. There seem to be fewer girls in Red House now. Kendall's bed stands where I last saw it, first on the right at the top of the aisle; Simone's is still opposite. Like the study the dorm is also familiar, but its differences are unsettling. Different quilts, different shoes beside the beds, different posters on the walls: Robert Pattinson and that boofy-haired kid from One Direction; others I don't recognise at all. There are even a couple of laptops on the bottom shelves of the bedside tables.

I stop at Red 12, my old bed. This area is sparser than the others, with a grey quilt thrown over a thin blanket. There aren't any posters on the brown wall, no photographs propped up beside the bed. I stare at the nametag, aware of the childish urge to rip it off. It's like walking past a house you once lived in and seeing someone else in your old bedroom. It feels like something has been taken from me.

I move to the windowsill. Grass and clusters of shrubs grow beneath the window. No dirt, no dust. Far off, over the roofs of other houses, the trees are taller, fuller. My eyes snag on Yellow House, tucked away against the road, and I grin, remembering how after lights-out Portia and I used to shine our torches at a window to piss off the girls sleeping inside their dorm. Only later did I find out it was Ruby's window, and after we'd become friends tormenting Yellow House wasn't so much fun anymore.

I haven't seen Ruby in a long time. We have lost touch. It's an odd expression: to lose *touch*. As though it was a cursory, careless mistake; more apt for describing a lost train ticket than a friend.

I sit on the edge of the bed. After Silver Creek, at the magnificent Big School on the edge of an azure bay, I had many friends. It was hard not to, when every day, almost every waking hour, I was surrounded by the girls and boys of my day house, Boyd. There we shared studies and common rooms and communal lunch. The days were long and full. After school there was sports practice or activities, like music club or hobbies. We ate dinner at school in the grand old dining hall, and afterwards went back to the house for evening prep. I never had a spare second to myself—from the moment I left home at 6.45 am to the crowded bus trip home, returning at 10 pm. We didn't have weekends free, either: every Saturday there was compulsory tennis or hockey or athletics.

After I finished school I went straight to university. I was seventeen years old. I had a place in Creative Arts at Melbourne University, and the subjects I was enrolled in, such as Writing Character and Film Noir, didn't sound like study at all.

Only a few friends from school joined me at university that year. Ruby had enrolled in a different degree, as had Simone (though she only stayed a semester before deferring) and another good friend, Marina. One or two were also living in the colleges on campus, which seemed to me like another version of school, with dormitories and communal meals. But most of my friends had taken a year off to work in boarding schools in the UK.

On the first day of university, one tutor asked everyone to introduce themselves. Many students mentioned what school they'd come from, but when it came to my turn, someone actually laughed when I told them the name of my school.

I felt myself blush to the roots of my hair. *What's so funny about that?* I wanted to ask. But my anger soon faded to something more docile: I felt like a fraud among these bearded, slightly pongy people. I wasn't a writer or a painter or a filmmaker. I wasn't *creative*. I loved literature, but I'd never written it. These students were arty, alternative—they had tattoos, wore fisherman pants and had piercings. They all seemed so much older than me, and they all appeared to know what they wanted.

During that first week students moved everywhere in groups of two or three or four. If only I could find someone else on their own, strike up a conversation, make a friend. But I was too shy to talk to anyone, and at the end of the second week, as I watched groups of boys and girls gather outside the lecture hall and head off together for coffee at the café outside the library, laughing and clearly already familiar with each other, I felt the first sharp pang of loneliness.

When I think back to university, I think of quiet. Long stretches of silence. Sometimes I would go a whole day without talking to anyone; I could sit through a tutorial and not say a word.

When I told Mum that I was having trouble making new friends, she shrugged and said, 'Don't worry about it. You've got lots of friends already.'

She didn't understand. What I'd had with most of my school friends—that hadn't been friendship at all. That had been the habit of the familiar, the reassurance of the unchanged. I was starting to learn that I wasn't good with change.

What is wrong with me? I used to wonder. I longed to have someone to grab lunch with from Union House, or to go for a beer with after lectures. Most days I ate my packed lunch on a windswept bench, before scurrying away to the library to watch French films borrowed from the vast VHS collection. I'd always liked my own company but this wasn't a happy kind of solitude. It felt as if something was absent, missing.

Sometimes I'd meet Ruby for afternoon tea. Other times I'd meet up with Marina for lunch at Tiamo on Lygon Street. We grew close during that first semester, hanging out most weekends. We were drawn together, I think, by our loneliness: while Marina had made one or two new friends, she'd never moved away from her family or their influence.

Over minestrone we'd talk about the future: after graduation, when we were working and living out of home. That was when life would begin; happiness was at the imaginary finish line. Marina would work in finance, earn big bucks. My ambitions were more watery—I wanted to write and work with words.

'And drive a sports car,' Marina laughed. 'We've got to have the matching sports cars.'

~

I'd never been all that interested in boys. I'd been on a few dates here and there, and I'd had a boyfriend for a couple of months in Year 11, but nothing more serious than that.

In my second year of uni, I started going out with Fraser. I'd met him through a school friend; they were in the same college. Fraser wore Ralph Lauren polo shirts and RM Williams boots, and he studied commerce.

I liked having a boyfriend. I liked to hear the words 'I have a boyfriend' coming out of my mouth. Fraser had even visited my parents' house a couple of times and met my mother. He had a car, a shiny ute, and we went out once a week for a meal or to a movie, and on Friday or Saturday night we'd go to the pub or a nightclub and get very drunk. I didn't really know how to talk to Fraser sober. In the mornings he'd drive me home. We never spoke much on these rides, and as we cruised over the West Gate Bridge, the oily water below, Fraser would lean forward to turn up the radio, Nova FM or the Fox, and I'd press my head against the warm window, a hangover pulsing behind my eyes.

Towards the end of the relationship I convinced myself that I loved him. Not with any burning passion, but because that is what you were supposed to feel for your boyfriend after six months together. I don't think he loved me—not at the end, anyway. We broke up over the phone after he told me he didn't want me coming to Noosa with him and his mate. But I didn't feel sad: it felt more like a breach of trust, as though he'd told someone a secret about me.

I didn't go out with anyone else for a long time. I wasn't interested in meeting new people. I felt cold, sexless. Occasionally I'd go out, get drunk and hook up with some guy, and whenever this happened I felt like I had moved outside of myself, watching what we were doing from high above. It was lonely, just like the tutorials.

~

At the time all of this was happening I had started reading *Mrs Dalloway* for one of my creative writing classes. One afternoon on the way home from uni, I read the passage where Clarissa walks through the garden at night, Sally Seton at her side, and Sally picks her a flower and kisses her.

The most exquisite moment of her whole life . . .

I put the book down. My hands had begun to shake and my face had flushed bright red. While Melbourne's industrial west flitted past in a blur of steel, I took a few deep breaths, glancing around the carriage to see if any other passengers had felt what I was feeling too—the urgent, intense realisation that this was what love was. This was what *my* love was.

But it didn't seem possible. Was I gay? How could I be? I was still living with my parents. Still in my old bedroom, with its single bed and rose-patterned wallpaper, practically unchanged since I was a girl. How would I ever find out?

I worked a few nights a week at a restaurant down on the waterfront called the Quarry. After a year or so, I had finally made a friend there—an Italian girl named Georgia, who had moved to Melbourne with her boyfriend. Georgia's English was patchy, and I had been teaching her bits and pieces during our shifts.

I liked Georgia. She stomped around the restaurant muttering in Italian about the customers, and every half hour she smoked angrily out the back by the cool room. She didn't like any of the other staff; I'd often catch her rolling her eyes at our boss. But she laughed uproariously at almost anything I said, even when I wasn't trying to be funny. 'Oh, Beckina,' she would sigh. 'You are wonderful.'

After our boozy staff Christmas party, a group of us headed into town. As the taxi crawled along Flinders Street, someone suggested we go to a gay bar—'For a laugh!'

We were dropped off outside a pub called the Stanley, in Collingwood. While the others went off to dance, Georgia and I sat on stools at the downstairs bar. Not the girlish mecca I had anticipated, the Stanley was full of steam, sweaty men and very tall transvestites.

'So, Beckina,' Georgia shouted over the music, 'why you not have a boyfriend?'

I laughed, toying with the coaster on the bar.

Georgia sucked on her cigarette. 'You like the woman? You lesbian?'

I shifted in my seat. 'I don't know.'

'But you come to this gay bar,' she remarked.

I nodded, gazing glumly into my pint. I'd drunk too much and now felt a bit sick.

Georgia nudged me. 'There is woman looking at you,' she said. 'She is cute, no?'

I glanced behind me. The girl Georgia had pointed out *was* cute, with dark curly hair. I began talking to her. I can't remember what about, maybe my studies, or her work—she was a chef at a café on Brunswick Street. An hour later we kissed.

I'd always imagined something would change inside me at that exact moment—fireworks would go off in the background, my confusion would be swept away and everything would be clear and sure. That it would be my Clarissa moment.

But it wasn't like that at all. I enjoyed the kiss, but I still felt the same detachment. The girl's lips were cold and soft, and she tasted of beer, as I'm sure I did. It felt more natural than kissing a boy, but only slightly. Then Georgia came over, took my arm. 'Come,' she said. 'Time to go home.'

I tried to block out what happened that night in Collingwood. Each time my thoughts strayed to the girl, I felt myself shudder, disgusted and afraid. Apart from Georgia, no one else knew—not Ruby or Marina, and especially none of the other girls from school. I'd been to parties where jokes about lesbians had been volleyed around the crowded room. Rug-munchers. Dykes. Vagitarians. There was always laughter in their voices, but venom too. No one would want to be my friend if they knew I went around kissing girls.

So I made a pact with myself: if I didn't speak about it, it would remain a half-live thing. If it was a secret, I could control it.

But as the weeks and months passed, something had reawakened in me, something from so long ago I had forgotten it was there, that took me all the way back to when I was a girl at Silver Creek. Some light, some fire. I couldn't stop thinking about girls—meeting a girl, kissing a girl, holding her in my arms. I wanted to fall in love. I wanted to be loved.

But the fear was still there too, and all the uncertainty that came with it. So it was that the desire for love split me in half. From that night I began to live two lives—one exploring this new and real part of myself; the other an act—until, after a while, I didn't know which one of me was telling the truth and which one was telling the lies.

12

~

There are no hikes this term. Instead we go out on community service, which is weekends of work on nearby farms and wineries, as well as projects around the school, like planting trees and building mud huts. I'm in a group with Simone, Lou and Emma. I'm so relieved I could weep.

Our first community service takes place at the Crawford farm. Mr Crawford is the local vet, and he treats every kind of animal: horses, sheep, cows, dogs. They have a few ponies on their small acreage, and Lou squeals with delight as we spot them grazing beside the drive.

After Mrs Crawford greets us out the front of the house, she leads us around the back to the shed with a barbecue and cleared space for our sleeping bags.

It's still early in the afternoon, and Emma and I pair up for the first jobs around the property. We muck out the stables and gather up stones in the paddocks so the horses don't trip and go lame.

We work until dusk. The night falls quick and fast, like a drop cloth. I wash my hands and arms and face at the tap behind the shed, my stomach growling. I can't wait to put the sausages on to the barbecue—and I'm about to announce to Emma that tonight I plan to break my sausage-and-bread record (eight servings) when Simone bursts into the shed.

'It's Lou,' she gasps. 'Oh my God . . .'

'What is it?' Emma drops the barbecue tongs into the dirt. 'What's happened?'

Simone bites her lip. 'I don't know. I just don't know if I should say.'

'Sim,' I say, 'you're scaring us. What's going on? Where's Lou?'

Simone gulps down some tears. 'She tried to hurt herself,' she finally says. 'While we were out, doing jobs, she starts getting really sad—crying and everything. She misses her family, and all her animals—and I think being here reminded her of home.' Simone wipes her nose with her sleeve. 'Anyway, just as it got dark, she walks away from me, towards a bunch of trees, and then . . . It was so awful . . . She just ran at this tree. Full pelt. She slammed right into it and then fell to the ground.'

Simone is crying in earnest now and Emma and I crowd around her for a hug. Afterwards I go outside to see if I can see Lou, circling the shed calling her name. I feel sick in my guts, like I've been punched. When I return, I volunteer to stay in the shed, in case Lou comes back. Emma leaves to find Mrs Crawford, and Simone has disappeared.

I linger by the barbecue, staring at the raw sausages. Simone and Emma have been gone for ages and I start to get scared. What if Lou is *dead*? What will we do? Then I hear murmuring on the other side of the tin and Simone walks in, Lou behind her. She is covered in dirt, her face bloated from crying.

~

Mrs Crawford ushers the three of us into the lounge room. She hands me the television remote. 'Watch whatever you like, dear,' she says. Then she goes down the corridor into another room and closes the door. Through the thin walls I can hear her talking on the telephone. Calling school, I suppose. Lou is somewhere else in the house. 'She's a little embarrassed about the whole thing,' Mrs Crawford had said. 'Giving us a fright like that.'

I switch on the TV. *Australia's Funniest Home Videos* is playing and we stare at the screen for a while. After a clip of a baby falling out of its bassinet, I finally ask, 'Is Lou okay?'

Simone clears her throat. 'She'll be fine. But only if no one else in Red House finds out about this.'

'What?'

'You have to promise that you won't tell anyone. Especially not Portia.'

I look at Simone. She is still straight-backed, and her eyes are glassy in the pink light. Beside her, Emma shifts uncomfortably on the couch. She doesn't trust me, I realise with a shock.

'Okay,' I mumble. 'I promise.'

'It's to protect her,' Simone says, her voice softer. She extends a hand to me, the black nail polish chipped, but she's too far away for me to reach.

~

Back at school, I sit on the edge of my bed, waiting for Miss Lacey's visit. For her to take the three of us aside for a talk, maybe even for a hot chocolate at her house, away from the rest of the house. I sit like this until lights-out and Miss McKinney screams, *Get in bed, Starford, or it's a Stonely Road for you and all.*

Miss Lacey doesn't come the next morning, either. When she wanders over at lunch for a chat with the girls at the other end of the table, she doesn't even look at Simone and me hardly touching our hamburgers. When Lou returns to school later that afternoon the silence has stretched like a wad of chewing gum.

'That's why we have to stick together,' Simone says bitterly. 'Because there is no way they're going to help us.'

I'm angry with Miss Lacey, but I'm also angry with Lou. This anger surprises me; I don't suppose it is fair. Shouldn't I blame myself more for what happened? I do feel like a bad friend not to have seen *how* unhappy she has been. I don't like feeling guilty—it's like a wave of white-hot panic.

But the more I think about it, the more opaque it becomes. Trying to make sense of why Lou hurt herself feels like falling into a pit of quicksand. When I was eight or nine years old, a girl from our street gassed herself in her family's car. She was sixteen. Her brothers went to my primary school, and when they came back after the funeral I expected them to be different. But they weren't—not on the outside, anyway. They still played footy at recess and ran about laughing on the oval at lunchtime. It was their mother who now moved through our town silently, her face grey and peculiar like she'd never smile again. 'You'd just *never* get over it,' I remember Mum saying. There was something rigid in her voice. And I kept wondering, every time I saw those boys, *But what about the girl? Who cares about what* she *felt?*

~

For the next community service we stay with Lou's grandmother. Her house, which is about an hour from the school, doesn't have any acreage attached, so there is no real work to do. Instead we ride around the backyard on a four-wheel motorbike and eat hot chips and Mars Bars from the corner store. No one says anything about what happened at the Crawford farm.

I'm surprised when Miss Lacey comes to collect us the next afternoon. Usually it is the assistants' job. The four of us line up on the verge, watching her park the Jeep. Lou is staying another night here, and when I say goodbye my eyes fill with tears. I'm afraid, even though I know Lou is happy with her grandmother.

She wraps her arms around me and I breathe in her familiar smell of earth and sweat and lavender. 'It's okay,' she murmurs. 'I'll see you tomorrow.'

'How was your weekend, girls?' Miss Lacey asks brightly when we've all climbed inside the Jeep.

We grunt a reply. Lou stands at the gate beneath a bush of tangled roses. The Jeep starts up with a rumble. Miss Lacey eyes us in the rear-view mirror, smiling.

'All's well that ends well, right?'

I meet her gaze, fighting the urge to lean over for a handful of her hair. Why doesn't she care? Sun blisters across the windscreen and we all wince. I twist in my seat to give Lou a final wave, but she has already gone back inside.

13

~

Exeat Weekend is the one weekend each term when we get to go home. From the balcony I watch the girls gambol down the hill towards the buses bound for Melbourne. In only a few hours they'll be watching television and eating decent food, far away from Silver Creek.

I'm not going home. Instead my parents are coming to me. We're staying in Riverfield, the small town near the school, in the motel next to the pub.

It'll be fun, Mum wrote in a letter. *We'll get to explore the area together.*

I can't believe my parents. Why would I want to stay so close to school? Why don't they understand these kinds of things like other parents do? I stared at the letter until the words blurred. I wanted to scream.

I didn't, of course. I picked up a lead pencil and wrote back, *That sounds nice xx*. It's a game we play now, my parents and me: never saying what we really think, never thinking what we say.

~

'Have you heard the one about the crab?'

'*Dad!*'

We're in the pub, empty except for two men at the bar mooching over pints of beer. In the background is a big-screen television playing the football. I had a steak for dinner, with fat chips and mushroom sauce. I wolfed the food down like I hadn't eaten in weeks, juice dripping from my chin.

'No?' Dad grins, sipping at his wine. 'Well, a man walks into a restaurant and says, "Waiter, do you serve crab?" And the waiter turns to the man and says, "Sir, we serve anyone."'

Archie glances at me from under his long lashes, chewing on a smile. I laugh, even though I've heard the joke a hundred times, and Dad joins in with a rasping chuckle.

Later that night, I snuggle in the narrow bottom bunk. The sheet and quilt are tucked in like a straightjacket and the blanket scratches at my chin. Mum appears out of the gloom, perching on the edge of the bed. I reach out for her warm hand. 'Good night,' she says.

The alcove where the bunks are smells like antiseptic. Stretching out, my toes poking from the end of the quilt, I think about what Portia said that morning. She wants us all to bring alcohol back from Exeat. 'For a party out the back,' she had said, laughing. 'Like normal teenagers.'

As everyone else headed to the buses, Portia had stayed with me out on the deck. It hadn't felt friendly, though, as she leant against the banister, chewing on a Redskin.

'Don't forget,' she said, pointing at me. 'Bring back whatever you can, I don't care if it's Grandma's sherry. But make sure you have something.'

My chest contracts with panic. Where am I going to find alcohol? Obviously my parents won't buy it for me, and I can't nick any from the stash of old liquor bottles under the sink at home. Portia will *hate* me if I don't bring anything back, and I'll lose everyone's respect. Then I remember the mud-brick huts, down past the hayshed. On community service a few weeks ago I'd seen crates of beer and wine down there—for the assistants, I suppose, who are partying while we're away. There are bound to be leftovers. I can sneak down when Mum and Dad drop me back to school.

I smile, rolling onto my side. The television from the next room casts a blue hue against the wall. I listen to the low murmur of my parents. It only takes a few minutes to fall into a thick, dreamless sleep.

~

I run my fingertips over my braces. They're coming off in a few months, the orthodontist said. As I push my bowl of cereal away, Archie wriggles his nose at me. He's only ten, but he's bigger than most boys his age, and every now and then I catch his look of surprise as he gets to his feet, alarmed at his newfound height. People forget Archie is still only a boy, and I feel a rush of love for him. He is sensitive; has been since he was tiny. Often, on the way home from primary school, boys hanging out at the milk bar call him *Red nob*. I've always been frightened of those kids, their leers and their dark eyes.

Everyone at Silver Creek calls me Bec now. Never Rebecca, or Starford—that didn't ever stick. I like Bec: there's a sharpness to it. Mum and Dad sometimes call me Becksy, which I only like when no one else is around, but mostly they call me Rebecca, which is starting to feel like a reprimand.

There were other names for me when I first came to the school three years ago. *Rabbit* was one, when the boys teased me about my teeth. *Bugs Bunny* and *Myxo mitosis* were others. I never told Mum and Dad about these names, or how they used to make me cry. I guess I shouldn't have smiled in that toothy way of mine, drawing attention to the gap between my big front teeth and my enormous overbite. Mum always said I have a nice smile. In the end, after all that teasing, I couldn't wait to get braces. But somehow, after I'd been to the orthodontist and my mouth was full of metal and aching, the teasing got worse.

'You were sleep-talking last night,' Archie says, head buried in his football almanac. 'Something about girls.'

I set down my spoon on the laminex table. 'Was not.'

'You were. Wasn't she, Mum?'

Mum drifts into the kitchenette. 'I didn't hear anything,' she says.

'But she was yelling!'

'Archie,' calls Dad from the ensuite. 'Finish your breakfast.'

'Hey, Arch,' I say when Mum has left the room again. 'Remember how *you* used to make sounds in your sleep? You know, how you used to rock?' I put my hands behind my head. 'You sounded like a total spaz.'

Archie sets his orange juice back on the table, his face pinched. It's years since Archie has rocked, but he still gets embarrassed about it. It was a strange, sleep-riddled chant where he drew himself up from the covers, crouching on his knees and rocking back and forth, moaning a single note over and over.

I smile. It's too easy to bait him; there's almost no fun in it. When he was small, four or five years old, Archie would regularly fly into rages at Dad, his blue eyes filling with tears as he stormed to his bedroom, slamming the door so hard it rattled the plaster in the hallway. A few minutes later a note was slipped under the door, *I HAT YOU DAD* scribbled in angry crayon.

Later Mum would coax Archie out of his room. As they sat together in the living room, flicking through the channels to find something on television, I couldn't help watching the way she held him, her brown arm wrapped around his tiny body, while her hand caressed the back of his neck. Her grip fierce yet her touch so soft.

~

Parked outside Red House, Dad offers to walk me to the front steps. I shake my head, grabbing my overnight bag. I can't speak—my teeth are chattering too much from the cold. Besides, if I speak I will cry, and I don't want him to see that. I don't want the girls inside to see it either. Their windows glow in the dark.

I feel like Alice in Wonderland, growing and shrinking in a single moment. Dad reaches over for a hug and the familiar bristle of his moustache and his faint sweaty smell make me want to fall against him.

'Well, Becksy,' he says, 'see you at the end of the term.'

I open the car door. Archie is asleep in the back, head lolling, his mouth open. The Bee Gees wafts through the speakers. I lean over to Mum, give her a kiss. She is leafing through her *Entertainment Book*, full of discounts, planning where they'll stop for dinner on the way home. 'Bye-bye,' she says, eyes fixed on the pages.

Back inside the bright dorm there is no time to cry. Girls are everywhere, galloping up and down the aisle with stories from Exeat, presents from their parents, news from the outside world about parties and footy matches and Geri leaving the Spice Girls. Grabbing my torch, I slip out the back door and run down the hill. I have about half an hour before anyone will notice I'm gone.

I am out of breath when I reach the huts, my side aching. I stumble around in the dark; my torchlight is already waning.

There are plenty of empty bottles scattered across the floor—wine, beer, whisky—but the crates are empty. I check each one for leftovers, but there are none.

I put my head in my hands. The hut stinks of old fire, and piss. What am I going to do? I can't go back empty-handed.

Near my feet is a small, empty bottle of Lemon Ruski. I shine the torch on the label, for a moment admiring the gold hammer and sickle. This would have to do.

~

Everyone has gathered around Portia's bed for the unveiling. Waiting for hush, she draws a bottle of bourbon and a bottle of red wine from a backpack, and there is a solemn murmur of admiration. Moving around the group, each girl reveals her booty. There is gin, brandy and even a bottle of port with an old rubber cork.

One more until my turn. Blood roars in my head. Portia smiles at me, the first real smile I've had from her in months.

'What have you got, Bec?'

All eyes are on me. 'Oh,' I manage to say. 'Bit of this, bit of that.'

'Well, come on then. Give us a look.'

I clear my throat. 'It's in my locker, actually. Show you later?'

'Let's have a look now.'

We stand up and walk towards the tog room. Just as I'm convinced that life is no longer worth living, a miracle comes in the form of Miss McKinney, spotted on the road. The girls scatter, stuffing the bottles in the drawers beneath their beds. 'Come on,' Miss McKinney calls from the doorway. 'Into bed and reading this instant.'

I expel a burst of breath. *Thank God*. Then I feel a cold hand clamp around my wrist.

'Show me,' Portia whispers. 'Quick.'

Before I can protest she drags me to the tog room. I stand at my locker, heart banging around my chest. Where the hell is Miss McKinney?

'Come on,' Portia snaps.

Nothing for it. I open the door, point to the bottom shelf where the Ruski bottle twinkles absurdly. 'There,' I mumble, moving to block the view. But Portia already has her foot out.

'Hang on,' she says. 'What *is* that?'

'Careful—'

But she's grabbed the bottle and holds it up to the light. She frowns and sniffs at the mouth.

'This is . . . water,' she says.

'No, it's not. It's vodka, good stuff. Try it if you don't believe me.'

The words are out before I can take them back. I slump against the door, my legs trembling. But Portia merely shrugs and hands it back.

'I've got more in my bag,' I say, my brain still haywire. 'Some gin too. Yeah, stole that from my parents. We can have that later, if you like?'

Portia laughs. It isn't a nice sound, and there is contempt in her eyes. She slinks off, around the corner, her sneakers scuffing the polish. When Emma comes out from the bathroom, she blinks into my open locker.

'Um, Bec,' she says, 'have you ever actually had a Lemon Ruski?'

I slam the door. 'Of course I have!' It's all very well for Emma—she managed to bring something back.

'Thing is,' she says, 'they're lemon flavoured, so they look sort of white-ish. Not clear, like that. And,' she adds, nodding at the bottle, 'they're usually sold with a lid on.'

I shrug. 'Like I said to Portia, I've already tried some and I threw the lid away.'

Emma stares. Her eyes are kind, reminding me of Mum. I turn away, embarrassed, as tears stream down my cheeks.

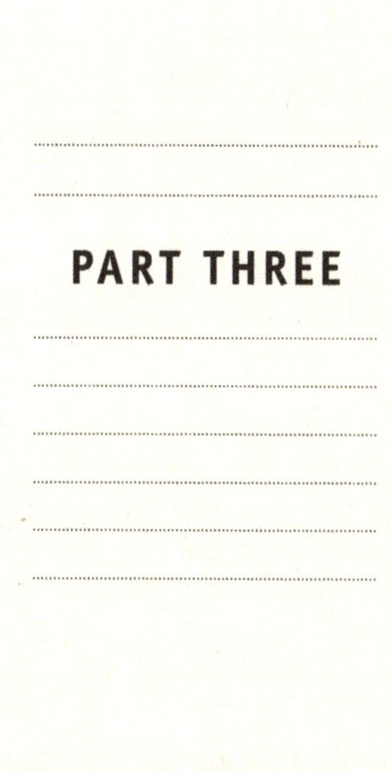

PART THREE

14

~

We're doing projects in History. I like learning about our past—about the Gold Rush and the Eureka Stockade, and the Boer War. I'm writing a letter from a convict, dated early 1800s. I don't know how convicts spoke or wrote back then, but I imagine their stationery was grubby so I stain the paper with dirt and tea and burn it around the edges to look like a scroll.

I feel different in the classroom: disciplined and hungry to learn as much as I can. I feel clever in these lessons, and that certainty, that confidence, is like a warm blanket. It still seems extraordinary to me how much is crammed into a single day up here.

In English we're reading *Romeo and Juliet*, and I'm enchanted by the lovers' doomed passion. So much, in fact, that instead of quiet reading I stand on my bed and shout lines around the dorm.

'Bloody hell, Bec!' cries Briohny from the corner. 'No one wants to hear your fucking sonnets!'

'They're not sonnets.'

'Whatever—shut up!'

'But don't you think it's wonderful?'

A few girls groan. In the next bed Emma makes a face. She is writing to Cadbury again: last term they sent her a whole box of complimentary chocolates after she complained a bar of Fruit & Nut had no fruit or nuts.

'Maybe it's time to consider other people in the dorm?'

I hadn't seen Miss Lacey standing in the doorway and her voice gives me a fright.

'I'm not hurting anyone,' I say with a pout.

'No, but you're disturbing silent reading.'

'So?'

'Oh Bec,' she says, tugging on the wisps of her hair. 'Why does everything have to be so difficult with you?'

But she sighs when my face falls and comes over to my bed. What Miss Lacey doesn't know is that I'd forgotten how much I love books, and how much of a reprieve they are from the chaos of Red House. 'Shakespeare *is* wonderful,' she says quietly. 'And it's great that you're enjoying reading the play. Miss Jones tells me you're doing very well in class.'

When she puts the lights out, I grab the torch and *Pride and Prejudice* from my bedside table. It's the tatty green leather-bound copy that used to belong to Nan. She gave it to me last year, after I watched the BBC series with Mum.

On the imprint page Nan had scribbled her name and the date, 1936. She was the same age then as I am now. It's strange to imagine Nan ever being young. She went to boarding school too. I wonder if she lay in bed at night, the lives of Elizabeth and Mr Darcy taking her far away from the dorm.

~

A girl from Purple House slit her wrists during the night. Her name is Helen. I don't really know her—she's not in any of my classes—but in Red House we've always called her Rapunzel, on account of her incredibly long hair.

It's all anyone can talk about at breakfast. Apparently Helen got out of bed after lights-out and cut herself in the bathroom. Then she walked back into the dorm bleeding everywhere, all the other girls screaming and crying, before she was rushed to the nurse.

I look over at Purple House's empty table. They don't have to go to class today. They might even get to go home.

'I'd cut my wrists if it meant I could go home,' Emma mutters.

'Double standards, isn't it?' I whisper, glancing towards Lou.

Emma chews on her nail and shrugs. 'What else is new?'

Later, standing in line for the crossie, I hear kids asking Helen's head of house about the blood and her wrists and how close to death she had been. Miss Constantine, a young, black-haired woman with a bird-like frame, scoffs. 'It would have taken her a week to bleed out,' she says. 'They were scratches, hardly deep at all. She was never in any real danger. I mean, she didn't even cut herself the right way!' She points to her wrist, makes a slashing movement along its length. 'You're supposed to cut *down* the inside of the forearm, not across the wrist.'

Red House is still talking about Helen as we get ready for bed. Why Helen did it doesn't seem to concern anyone; they're all more interested in *where* she did it—and how the girls in her house were driven home in a bus that afternoon.

'She should have done it at the chapel,' Portia says. 'Then it could have been religious, like a sacrifice. She should have strung herself up to the cross, slit her wrists and hung there like Jesus. We all would have seen her as we walked down to breakfast.'

The dorm has gone quiet.

'That's horrible, Portia,' Simone says. 'How can you say that?'

But Portia just cackles.

I climb into bed and pull the covers to my chin. I am thinking about Lou, of course, but also about Kendall. What if she tries to hurt herself?

Portia looks around, smiling slyly. 'Rapunzel, Rapunzel,' she sighs.

That night I dream about the lambs in the front paddock. They bleat sadly as Portia shepherds them towards the chapel. At the altar they're hoisted to the top of the giant crucifix where their throats are cut by figures dressed in black. I cry out, but no sound comes from my mouth. Blood drips down the crucifix and the lambs' wool falls in a soft coil.

~

The next morning I wake up with stoney dread in the pit of my stomach. Tomorrow we're heading out on our house hike. To distract myself, I think about home—about Mum and Dad and Archie, our warm living room with the soft glow of the television, my bed. If only I could have a short break from Silver Creek, a few days is all I would need. But I can't.

In the afternoon I visit the nurse, pretending to have gastro. There is a chance, if she believes I'm sick, that I'll be sent home: it's been happening ever since a boy contracted meningitis. But as she takes my temperature she frowns, and I know I haven't fooled her. She gives me charcoal tablets, watches me swallow down a couple with a gulp of cold water. 'There,' she says. 'That will set you right for the hike.'

God, I write in my diary that night, *four days with the house is going to be hard.*

The next morning, I pile into a Jeep with six other girls. Two more vehicles follow in convoy. Rain spits against the windows. An hour later we stop at an unfamiliar site. No one seems to want to get out.

'Come on,' Miss Lacey says, but even she sounds reluctant, peering through the window at the murky sky.

The rain doesn't stop all day. It's proper rain, too, stirring up an earthy smell from the ground.

After we set up camp no one can get a fire started. I'm so hungry I eat my tinned beef and vegetables cold. Emma watches, horrified, until eventually she cracks open the lid of her own tin. 'It's not too bad,' she says through a mouthful.

I hunt through a bag of scroggin for a dried apricot. 'I wonder if we'll look back and think these are the best days of our lives?'

'Doubt it. Why do they always say that about school, anyway?'

'Teachers say it, don't they?'

'Figures,' Emma says, grinning suddenly. 'They've come back to work at school!'

We look at each other and fall about laughing. I don't know what we're laughing about, but it doesn't matter. When Emma wipes her eyes, smearing beef across her cheek, I think, *Thank God I have you.*

~

We hike through sleet. Wind flays at any bare skin. I can't feel my hands. The terrain is slick, with exposed roots and loose rocks—a few girls have fallen already. We're headed for a hut somewhere on the other side of the mountain, with a loft and a giant fireplace. The only thing that keeps me going is imagining that warm glow against my face.

On a ridge the group stops for photographs in front of an enormous boulder. Teeth chattering, Emma links her arm through mine. Miss Lacey shouts, 'Cheese,' for each snap.

We arrive at the hut just as the sun drops. From a distance it looks like a hunting cabin from a horror film, with a shadowy porch and even an animal skull fixed above the door. Inside it smells dusty and faintly smoky from a pile of old ashes in the fireplace.

Portia and her group move swiftly towards the loft. I follow up the ladder, my pack swaying. At the top they're already laying down their mats and sleeping bags, and when I edge towards the corner Portia blocks my way.

'What are you doing?' Beanie off, her greasy hair sticks out at odd angles.

'Just setting up my mat.'

'No room.'

I point to the corner. 'There's a spot right there.'

Sarah pushes past. 'There's no room, Rebecca. Get it?'

Portia turns away, leaving me to stare at the back of her head. It's so stuffy up here—I can feel sweat gathering above my lip. I close my eyes. *If you let me sleep here,* I will her from across the loft, *I won't bother you again. I won't talk to you or offer you food or try to make you laugh, I promise. Just please give this final thing to me.*

But I don't have the courage to say it. When Portia looks at me again, she asks, 'Why are you still here?' in the same tone she might use to ask someone to pass her a pillow. As if this cruelty was nothing to her, just part of her day. Now the words come gushing from my mouth.

'Why are you *being* like this?'

Everyone stops and turns. Portia's eyes widen a fraction. She takes a step towards me, her fists clenched.

'Can you just fuck off?' she says, pointing to the ladder.

I peer over the edge. Emma is standing at the bottom, hands on hips. 'I've saved you a spot here,' she calls.

'See?' Portia says. '*Your* friends are down there.'

My knees buckle and I shift the weight of my pack. Sarah has positioned her sleeping bag next to Portia. 'It'll be you soon,' I say to her—what do I have to lose now? 'And then someone else, and someone else. And then no one will be left.'

From the corner Briohny sniggers, twirling a finger around her ear. Portia covers her mouth, eyebrows lost in her fringe. She's laughing at me.

~

Dinner is jaffles and tinned spaghetti. After the utensils are washed and dried, Miss Lacey gets the fire going. A few girls sit at the table near the door, drinking cocoa and telling stories. For some reason Simone has coloured her face with black soot from the hearth. A white shoelace is tied around her head.

I sit in front of the fire. Later we're going to roast marshmallows. I'd been looking forward to it.

Miss Lacey rummages in the woodbin for another large log, tossing it on the fire, then takes a seat beside me, resting her chin in her hands. Her hair smells of strawberries. 'What's the matter, Bec?' she asks. 'You've hardly said a word the whole hike.'

Her eyes are soft in the firelight. I fiddle with my watch, glancing around the hut. Everyone is having a good time—even Kendall, perched at the bottom of the ladder, is chuckling at soot-faced Simone.

'I'm fine,' I say, staring at the flames. 'Just tired.'

Miss Lacey frowns, her mouth a straight line. 'Are you sure?' she asks, searching out my eyes. But she doesn't push it.

~

I lie awake for hours, watching the light glow green at the window. Once or twice a few girls shift in their sleep. Just as I'm drifting off, a long, low fart rumbles around the alcove. I'm sure it was Simone—I'd know her farts anywhere—and when I start laughing tears come too.

I wake around dawn, alert and claustrophobic. Grabbing my boots, I creep out of the hut and head towards a crop of rocks nestled beneath a few eucalypts. With the mist clearing I can see across the valley to the Razorback Road, the range of knolls jagged like teeth, and Hell's Kitchen beside it, with a rock face descending into thousands of tangled blackberry bushes at the base of the mountain. All of a sudden there is an eruption of pink and orange and red as the sun rises, so enormous I feel like I could reach out and touch it.

I hear a twig snap. Portia is walking towards me, her camera slung over her shoulder. She looks like a convict with her wild hair and striped pyjama pants.

'Hey, loner,' she calls.

I wait for the others to join her. But she is alone. She scrambles up the boulder and we sit together in silence. I sense her fidgeting beside me, her thermals scratching at my arm, and then I hear the shutter click as she takes a photo of me. I don't know what to do or say, but somehow I manage to give her a withering look.

She lowers the camera, frowning. 'What?' she says. And then: 'Wish you'd been up in the loft last night.'

My heart flickers at this, my palms growing sweaty against the cool moss. I almost turn to her, to see if she means it. But I am starting to understand that knowing Portia is a bit like grasping at smoke.

I tilt my face towards the sun, feeling something leech out of me. Behind us come voices. I take a deep breath. If only I could have a few more minutes sitting like this, with Portia quietly at my side. If only I could hold on to this moment where for once I feel like I am in control. But now I hear footsteps on the verandah and the steps, and I turn back to the sunlight as girls begin making their way through the tall grass.

15

~

The cold is relentless. More girls get sick, and a few are even sent home for long stretches. Everyone is gaunt and miserable-looking, with runny noses. During the day my lower back aches, right where my tailbone nudges against the chair.

One night, as we lie in bed with our breath hanging above our faces, Miss McKinney scolds us for talking. Since I was sent to the science labs, Miss McKinney—or *Butterball* as we now call her—always seems to be telling us off for misdeeds such as taking too long in the showers or not tidying our beds. I'm looking forward to a new assistant arriving from France next week. Her name is Miss Sagnier and she will help out in my French class.

'Not another peep,' Miss McKinney says, flashing her torch over the beds. 'Got it?'

'Sure,' I call in a high-pitched voice. '*Butterball*.'

Miss McKinney freezes in the doorway. 'Who said that?'

Girls are laughing now, shamelessly. I roll on my side and close my eyes. Give it a minute and she'll go. But she doesn't. Instead she says, 'Right. If that's the way it's going to be, get out of bed, all of you.'

'What? No way!'

Miss McKinney switches on the dorm lights. 'I said get out now or I'll send the lot of you to Mr Pegg.' She raises a hand to her forehead, like a salute. 'I've had it up to here. You girls need to be taught a lesson.'

She marches us outside, ordering us to stand in a line on the road. I'm only wearing an old T-shirt and a pair of long johns.

'Now,' Miss McKinney says, 'let's see how you like it out here for a while.'

'Are you crazy? It's the middle of winter!'

Miss McKinney comes over, sizing me up. Up close her face is actually rather pretty, with small dark freckles and sharp green eyes. 'Well, Starford,' she says, 'maybe you need to learn when to shut the fuck up.'

She walks off, down the road, and disappears into the gloom. Minutes drag by. When we realise she isn't coming back, girls crouch over their knees, blowing into cupped hands. Further up the line I hear someone crying.

'Why didn't you just own up, Bec?' Briohny says. 'You're so selfish.'

I stare into the black and starry sky, grinding my teeth until my jaw aches. Maybe I should have owned up? I shake my head. No one else would have. I glance along the road. It's laughable, this situation—sixteen girls standing on the road in the middle of the night, in the middle of winter—but I can only marvel at my own rage, my blistering desire to pick up a rock and sink it into Miss McKinney's fat head.

Finally we are allowed back to bed, but no one sleeps well. The next morning my cough has returned; it's deep in my chest now, dry and rasping.

~

Each Thursday that term we have electives. I sign up for the cross-country ski team. There are eight of us—four girls and four boys. No one else from Red House is in the squad and I don't know the other girls. But they seem to know each other, and huddle together in a friendly trio.

The squad trains at the foot of Mount Franklin. Miss Constantine is our coach. She is strict with the exercises, screeching during time trials and reproaching us whenever we lag behind.

'So how are things in Red House?' she squawks during a break one afternoon. 'Planning any more dorm raids?'

She laughs. It's a horrible sound, like nails down a blackboard. The rest of the squad rearrange their skis, not looking at me. I'm not likely to get any sympathy—Red House's exploits haven't exactly made us popular around the campus.

I gaze behind Miss Constantine to the cluster of pines behind a wire fence, curling and uncurling my fingers inside my gloves. I'd love to say all kinds of nasty things to her, but I'm dwelling on how stupid it is to have barely spoken a word to anyone all afternoon. I'll never make any new friends if I keep up like this. I hadn't realised until now that this was something that I wanted, and for a moment the loneliness stings like a cut. Then I smile to myself. After being so desperate to get away, I'm now looking forward to seeing the Red House girls when I get back to school.

~

Mr Pegg visits the house. He stands in the doorway, so tall his head nearly touches the frame. Miss McKinney has told him about the other night.

'I'm disappointed, girls,' he says. He thought our childish behaviour would have come to an end by now. 'And as punishment you'll all camp for a night on Dusty Hill.'

'That's really all they've got, isn't it?' Emma sighs. 'Sleeping in tents.'

But another surprise awaits us. The next morning Miss Lacey gets everyone out of bed early, and leads us to a damp and slightly metallic-smelling classroom beside the science labs.

Father Wilson stands at the front of the room. When everyone has taken a seat, he hands around sheets of paper, which are in fact photocopies of recent death notices in the newspaper.

'Now,' he says, rocking back on his heels, 'I've got a task for misbehaving girls like you. I want you to take your pencils and I want you to circle every letter *e* in these notices. Every mistake means you must do it again, and no one leaves until the last girl is finished.'

I glance down and wince. A lot of people died last week.

I start scratching away at the paper. Next to me Simone doodles in the corner of the page. Feeling a nudge, I look sideways and see her giving me one of her crafty smiles. I nod and her pencil soon clatters to the floor.

'Oh my God! I can't believe it!'

She pushes her chair away, stands up, then sits down, throwing her arms across the desk.

'Simone,' I say in my best actress voice, 'what on earth is the matter?'

'That's my uncle,' she cries. 'Edward Martin. I knew he was sick. The doctors said he had longer—a year, maybe more. But he hasn't made it. And now . . . and now you're making me circle letters in his *name* . . .'

Briohny jumps to her feet. 'This is crazy!' She takes the sheet of paper and scrunches it into a ball. 'I'm going to tell my parents about what you've made us do. This is like . . . child abuse.'

'Now look here . . .' The colour is draining fast from Father Wilson's face.

There is a knock at the door and he strides across the room. Through the doorway I glimpse Miss Lacey. When Father Wilson returns to the blackboard, he looks sheepish.

'I think we'll finish up the exercise there,' he says quietly. 'So you can get to breakfast.'

But I've lost my appetite. I toss my paper aside, pocketing the pencil. 'What a crock,' I sigh.

Simone nods, handing Father Wilson her sheet. There's a sketch of a penis in the corner.

'I just want you to know,' she says, twirling a lock of dark hair around her ear, 'I was only kidding about my uncle.'

Father Wilson peers down at the paper, his mouth opening a fraction. But before he can say anything Simone has fled, grabbing my hand as she streaks past, our laughter rattling down the stairs.

~

It is a free afternoon. Unused to spare time, most girls lounge around the dorm. I think about writing a few letters, but my pencil and paper sit untouched on my desk. My letters home have grown infrequent: whenever I sit down to write I can never think of an original thing to say. *Went for a run today. Had a pretty gross dinner tonight. It's cold up here, still* . . . Mum and Dad must be bored to death by them.

Someone suggests going for a walk behind the house. Portia, I notice with some alarm, brings along the axe. We stop after ten minutes of bush bashing, and while a few girls sit in the dirt and smoke a cigarette I kick through the tall grass, bending over to peer at rocks and flowers and pellets of animal poo on the ground. I breathe in the nature smell, feel it cold and expanding in my throat.

There are, of course, things I could write home about, things my parents wouldn't really understand. Like how quiet and unmoving it is out here, in a way it never is in the city, and how this means you can hear everything, especially your own thoughts, clear as a penny down a well. How my senses have sharpened, grown keen. How I feel more liberated and ungoverned and irresponsible, because we're in the middle of the bush, while the rest of the world, in offices and shops and schools, keeps turning without us. How rules and discipline just seem pointless when you feel more *animal*.

Portia comes up beside me, still brandishing the axe. 'It's so great out here,' I say. 'Don't you think? Peaceful.'

Our bare arms touch. Her skin is soft and warm, and I can smell her sweat, which always reminds me of meat left out of the fridge. She picks at a piece of bark, studies it. 'I never really like being in the bush on my own,' she says. 'When I was little, my family went camping by a river, and my brothers found a wombat hole. They told me there was a present inside, so I got down on my tummy and wriggled in. I got stuck, of course. Then my brothers thought it would be funny to tell me to keep still because a snake was slithering towards me . . .'

She lights a cigarette, squinting at the end. This is the first time she has confided in me in ages. I wait for her to go on, but she doesn't.

'That's not very nice,' I say carefully.

Portia glances at me before her eyes slide back towards the bush. 'It was a long time ago.'

'I'm terrified of snakes too,' I say. 'Ever since I was a girl.'

She smiles. 'Yeah?' Then she points. 'I want to chop down a tree.'

I blink at this non sequitur. Sometimes, talking to Portia, I feel like I am falling down a crevasse—she is so unpredictable. 'For firewood?' I say.

She laughs, slapping me on the back. 'No, dickhead. For fun.'

I stand under some wattle while she searches for the best tree. From this distance the girls look different, as if for the first time I'm seeing them in full size. Everyone is filthy, hair lank and dull in the grey light.

At last Portia selects a mid-sized white gum, about ten metres tall, with smooth and weirdly skin-like bark. She sizes up the tree, half squatting with her legs apart, before drawing the axe over her shoulder and bringing it down with a tremendous *thunk*.

'Your turn, Bec,' she calls.

I stay under the wattle, hands deep in my pockets. There is something not right about chopping down a gum.

'What are you scared of?' Portia laughs. 'It's just a tree.'

The girls are watching me. 'I'm not scared,' I sigh, edging forward.

Portia hands me the axe. It is warm in the smooth groove where her hands have been. 'Just give it a few chops,' she says.

The axe is heavy, and old. A few times I've been chopping wood and the head has flown right off. Usually I enjoy cutting the firewood. It is calming, methodical, splitting down the centre, on the line.

I draw back and swing. The trunk is thin but surprisingly sturdy, and the tree reverberates like a tremor through my body. I drop the axe and the girls laugh. I expect Portia to make fun of me, but she gestures for me to come closer.

'Your technique is wrong,' she says. 'You need to stand with your legs further apart, side on, and make sure you bend your knees. Here.'

She stands behind me, grasping the axe in front, indicating for me to put my hands on the handle too. We strike at the tree a few times. She is so near I can feel her breath on my neck. Why is she standing so close?

I'm aware of the other girls watching us, their faces strange. For so long—the whole year, just about—I've wanted this nearness, this proximity, but now having it only makes me want to scream.

Briohny sniffs, spits. 'That's so gay,' she says, which earns a laugh.

After other girls have had a turn, Portia makes the final strike. The tree shudders, tilting. We all watch, hands on hips.

'*Timber!*'

The gum arcs and plummets like an explosion, bringing down half-a-dozen other small trees and shrubs. Birds scatter from everywhere, shrieking across the sky.

'Fuck,' Portia breathes. Then we're jumping up and down. We've cut down *a tree*. Jubilant, I pump my fist in the air until I feel her again at my side, reaching up to grab my hand.

~

I tell Emma I like Rich Browne. I make her swear not to tell anyone. I don't know why—it's not true. He is smarmy and skinny and not very bright. When I write in my diary *I love RB* my hand feels heavy. But I suppose I should start liking boys more and Rich Browne seems like a safe choice: I know he has absolutely no interest in me. Still, I do wonder what it must be like to go out with someone. To like them enough to want to kiss them all the time, and talk to them in your free time.

Next to the chapel is a cluster of bushes where couples go to kiss after dinner. It's right near the path leading to Red House. We all know how the girl and boy stand together under the orange light near the doors, looking shifty, before slinking into the shadows. I can't understand why it's such a popular spot—there isn't even anywhere to sit. If I wanted to kiss someone, I would take them to the platform above the dam, where it's quiet and you can see the moonlight on the water, and the old gum tree creaks in the reeds.

One night Simone and I spy on some kissing. Lately it seems all Simone can talk about is boys and kissing. The current obsession is Greg, a sandy-haired boy in her Japanese class. I don't see the appeal, but what do I know? I've kissed only two boys in my life. My first was an unpleasant kiss inside a cupboard during school camp and the second was after a date with a boy named Stephen to the Hoyts Megaplex followed by a value meal at McDonald's.

Simone and I hide behind a bush. A moment later the boy and girl come into view. Leila from Jade House and Tom from Blue House. Beneath the halo of light, they make an attractive couple. Leila has dark hair and olive skin, while Tom is tall and blond. Tom shuffles his boots, looking past her to the stone wall with strange intent. Then they come together, arms loose around one another's waists, and begin kissing. It seems effortless, this desire.

'He's so hot,' Simone whispers, wriggling closer. 'Look at his arms!'

'Mmm,' I say. But I'm not looking at him. I'm looking at Leila. It's like I am in a trance; I can't take my eyes off her. How have I never noticed how shiny her hair is, draped long and loose down her back? Or the soft line of her jaw? It's freezing, but she is wearing a T-shirt, which clings to her—to the swell of her breasts—as her thin wrists loop tighter around Tom's waist. Wondering what it would feel like to be pressed against her, I immediately blush.

Eventually they break off. Their timing is perfect. They speak together quietly, Tom with his hand on Leila's hip. Then he leaves, Leila watching him go before she too heads back down the track towards her house.

Simone and I clamber out from the bushes. She slings her arm over my shoulder, laughing. 'Enjoy that did you, creep?'

I shrug her off. 'You're the creep!'

'Relax, I'm only joking.' She moseys on, gazing at the starry sky with the same dreamy expression. 'I mean, Tom is good-looking, but there are bigger hotties at the school, don't you think?'

I glance down the hill to the cluster of girls' houses, where I can make out a bluish smudge. Somewhere a light goes on, burning bright through the dark.

16

~

New assistants arrive as the old ones leave. We have a gathering to farewell Miss McKinney. Miss Lacey brings cupcakes with pink icing and a packet of jelly snakes, and a bottle of lemonade makes its way around the study.

I can't wait to meet the new assistants. Two young women from France and Canada, and three men from Scotland, Germany and England. There is much speculation about what they will look like and what kind of people they will be.

The following night they're all seated at the teachers' high table. It's a merry meal—I can see empty bottles of wine lining the slush trolley. Miss Lacey is chatting with the Scottish assistant, Mr Connolly, a gangly man with curly hair, every now and then putting her hand on his arm and throwing her head back to laugh.

'I think Miss Lacey might have a new boyfriend,' Portia sneers. 'Hamish McDougal . . .'

A few of us look towards the high table, and when Miss Lacey gives a small wave Portia makes kissy faces.

'Why would she be interested in him?' I say. 'He's not even good-looking.'

'He's not that bad,' says Emma. 'It's not like she has a lot of choice up here, anyway.'

I chew on a piece of bread. I don't see why she has to have a boyfriend at all.

Sitting beside Miss Lacey, dressed in a pink polar fleece, is the French assistant, Miss Sagnier. She is very pretty, with chestnut hair and honey-coloured skin. She eats her dinner slowly, probably horrified at the gristly stew, having just come from the land of fois gras and champagne.

I'm still thinking about Miss Sagnier the following night as I'm standing at the bathroom sink brushing my teeth. I hope we become friends.

At the next basin Portia begins dragging the comb through her short hair. For once she has wrapped a towel around herself. Ronnie and Briohny stand nearby, waiting for showers.

'I had the weirdest dream last night,' Portia murmurs. 'I dreamt I kissed Leila from Jade House.'

I think I've heard wrong. The bathroom has gone very quiet. I want to look at Ronnie and Briohny, but I keep my eyes on the shiny taps.

'It was weird,' Portia continues, her comb clattering in the sink. 'We were walking down to dinner, and then we were in the trees. There were other people around, I think. And then I just kissed her. For ages.'

I spin around, still not believing what I'm hearing. Panic bats at my stomach. Are they playing some sort of trick on me? But Ronnie just stands there fidgeting with her bottle of shampoo, while Briohny stares at the ceiling as if it is the most interesting thing in the world.

'Then what happened?' I splutter through the toothpaste. Ronnie and Briohny glare at me, but turn to Portia, waiting for a reply.

She shrugs. 'We kissed more. It was . . . nice.'

'But you don't . . . I don't know . . . like her or anything, do you?' Ronnie says. 'I mean, what about Rollo?'

'What about him?'

Ronnie blinks several times. 'Don't you still like him?'

Briohny still hasn't spoken. Her lip is slightly curled, nose pinched. 'It was just a dream,' she says. 'It doesn't mean anything.'

'But that's what I've been wondering.' Portia sighs. 'I mean, with my mum and everything . . .'

We all look at the floor now, suddenly embarrassed at this conflation.

'I've heard it skips children. That every third child has it.'

'Has *what*?'

Portia turns back to the mirror, gripping the bench. Colour has crept up her arms, flushing across her chest. This is the first time I've ever seen her vulnerable, I realise with shock. I'd always imagined I'd enjoy it, but it doesn't feel good to see her like this—instead I feel sorry for her.

'You know,' she finally replies. 'The gay gene.'

'You're not . . . *gay*!' Ronnie explodes. 'That's just crazy!' She looks to Briohny again, almost imploring her to agree.

'Just a dream,' Briohny says.

Portia smiles without feeling. In the reflection she meets my eye, holds it.

The showers are free. Briohny and Ronnie glance at each other again, something passing between them, before locking themselves in adjacent cubicles. Steam soon fills the bathroom.

I wonder if I should say something to Portia—something to make her feel better, to show her that I understand. She looks so small, standing there on the cold tiles in just a towel, and so *unhappy*.

But I say nothing. How can I trust her not to wield her own shame against me? I wipe the toothpaste from my chin and walk past her, my eyes fixed to the tiles. I can't risk her recognising those same feelings in me.

~

Miss Sagnier is on prep duty that night. When I ask for some help with my French, she takes me into the dorm and we sit on my bed while she explains the various conjugations of *être*. She smells nice, like the hand cream Mum uses.

'Isn't she great?' I gush afterwards, back at my desk.

Simone swivels in her seat. 'She's okay.'

'Don't you think she's pretty?'

Simone frowns. 'You're being weird.'

But she doesn't understand. In French class, the boys stare at Miss Sagnier openly. At her arms and legs and breasts and bum. They think she's hot, which gives them some sort of permission to look at her like this. I wish I could look at her like that—like it was something I was allowed to do. Instead I take her in patiently, and sometimes when her eyes meet mine she will smile, like we're sharing something, like I'm not doing anything wrong.

I start to wonder: is this desire? How can it be? But I don't have another word for it. I walk back from class on my own, trying to take apart the threads of these feelings, only managing to work them back into a tighter knot. I think of Portia, and her dream about kissing Leila. No one has mentioned it again. I wonder if Portia looks at Miss Sagnier like I do, thinking what I think. The idea is disturbing.

I know the rest of the house doesn't feel like this. I know they *like* Miss Sagnier, but they don't go red whenever she talks to them, or get sweaty palms and a thick voice. They might think she's pretty, but they're not excited by that beauty; it doesn't make them anxious or uncomfortable. They don't want to be with her when she isn't around, and they don't long to have her looking at them. These feelings they have around boys, never girls.

I wonder what would happen if I told someone—that I like Miss Sagnier like a girl likes a boy. What would they say? I try to picture myself telling Emma or Simone, but I can never see past those first words. But I can see their faces; I can see their surprise, swiftly followed by disgust. I know it would feel like deceit for me to admit to such a thing. To have pretended to be one thing when I am another. And yet, despite this fear, this secrecy, there is a new feeling growing inside me. Something private, but something sure, like a buoy in a deep, dark sea.

~

One afternoon, when everyone is back from a long run, covered in mud and soaked through from the rain, Portia wanders into the dorm. After her confession in the bathroom, I've avoided being alone with her. But I can't stop thinking about what she said, and what my own feelings must mean. At first I felt certain in them, but now I am afraid.

Portia's had a shower and is naked again, and begins to get dressed beside her bed with the usual languor. I'm reading a letter from my parents. I'll shower later, after I've been down to the tuckshop to buy a packet of Tim Tams.

'What are you staring at?'

I look up. Portia is pointing a finger in my direction, her pupils shrunk to pinpoints. But it is Emma, clipping her toenails, who replies, 'What?'

'You were watching me get dressed,' Portia says. 'That's *what*.'

She has made her way across the floor and is standing in the middle of the aisle, her pubic hair bristling.

'God,' she cries. 'She's still looking!'

I laugh now, I can't help it. 'Portia, you are walking around naked. It's a bit hard not to.'

She turns on her weathered heels, seizing my words. 'You were looking too?'

I blush. 'No, of course not.'

'What are you—a dyke? Are you a dyke?' She spits the words out.

Emma puts aside her clippers. 'What are you on about?'

'But Bec,' Portia persists, now gesturing at me. 'You did see her looking at me, didn't you? You saw her perving on me.'

'Eww,' Briohny cries from across the room. 'That's gross.'

Emma shakes her head. But taking in all the shocked faces, she turns to me, a little fearful. 'Bec?' she says. 'Tell her.'

The dorm is unmoving. My breath sounds loud. 'Well . . .' I begin.

At the back of my head is the dim possibility of Portia playing a trick. But seeing Ronnie's and Briohny's cold stares from across the dorm freezes this suggestion in my throat and my mind goes blank. All I can see is Miss Sagnier and her smile. The warm weight of her slender arm—or Leila's, or any girl, really, because it is now clear to me that it is, and perhaps always will be, *a girl*—around my waist. My own fumbling longing. And then I think with a panic how they all must see it, the girls, as they wait for me to defend my friend. They must see everything written all over my face, and I suddenly feel so foolish, so naïve, to have imagined I could ever really live like that, have those kinds of feelings about girls, in the real world.

'I don't know,' I stammer. 'I didn't see.' I wave the letter pathetically. 'I was *reading*.'

'You didn't *see*?' Emma says. 'What the fuck, Bec?'

My hands start shaking. I want to close my eyes and lie down. Nothing seems to be holding me together anymore; I feel so brittle I'm worried I might fall over and break in half.

'You know,' Portia says, swaggering back towards her bed, her white bottom quivering with each step, 'I've seen Emma watching us get dressed before. I didn't want to say anything at the time.' She picks up her talcum powder and taps a cloud of it to her pubes. 'I mean, we can't have a *lesbian* in the house with us.'

'Are you guys retarded?' Emma shouts. 'I am not a lesbian. I wasn't looking at her. I've *never* looked at anyone like that!'

'But I saw you,' Portia says, dusting her hands clean. 'There's no use lying.'

'This is crazy.' Emma grabs her towel. 'You guys are insane, all of you. I seriously cannot wait until this year is over and I never have to see any of you again!'

Like a pack of dogs, the house stirs, brays. But Emma has already charged off to the bathroom. No one goes after her.

I sit on the end of my bed, something coiling around my insides, tugging. Why didn't I defend her? When I glance across the dorm and see how Portia looks at me, like she's proud, that tug grows more insistent, and more painful.

~

I don't see Emma again until dinner. I try to draw her aside before line-up, but she shrugs me off. 'Seriously, Rebecca,' she says. 'Don't even look at me right now.'

After prep, I follow her into the tuck room. I know it's probably making her madder, but I can't help myself. I have to fix this.

She doesn't say anything at first, just goes through the motions of making a cup of tea. Stirring in the milk, she finally turns to me, her face pale under the harsh lights.

'I don't care what they say about me,' she says. 'They could say I fucked an emu and I wouldn't bat an eyelid. But you . . .' She bangs about in the cupboard and brings out a sachet of sugar. 'I'm one of the only people who cares about you here. And you *still* didn't stand up for me.'

'I'm sorry,' I say. 'I fucked up.'

My mouth feels gluey, words like tissue stuck to the sides. I can't look at her. I'm terrified that I've ruined our friendship, and that fear makes me want to drop to the floor and howl. I remember how, when I was a kid, I climbed my parents' antique wardrobe, hoping to find some treasure at the top. As I gripped that high ledge, there had been a split second when I felt the wardrobe tilt, just enough time to register profound regret, before the whole thing came crashing down on top of me.

'Do you hate me now?' I whisper.

Emma rolls her eyes. 'Don't be such a dickhead.' She leans against the bench. 'I'm angry, really angry. I need some time away from you.' When she turns back, her face is a little softer. 'You're far from perfect, Bec. But you've also got so much going for you—you're the smartest girl I know. But really—' she brushes by, turning out the lights on her way—'when are you going to stop being so fucking *weak*?'

17

~

The dorm has turned cold after dark clouds moved across the sky. I check my watch and I realise I've been sitting here on the bed for ages—I shouldn't really linger like this, I have to keep moving. But my head feels foggy, like I've just woken from a nap.

In the tog room, the lockers and metal crates are filled with clothes and crusty-looking camping gear, hiking boots stacked like milk bottles on the top shelves. It's even colder in here, and smells of mould.

My old locker looks the same, just a few more scuffs around the handle, some chipping at the bottom, at the ridge. I can still see myself crouched here all those years ago, unpacking with Mum. She had spent weeks sewing labels into my clothes—every sock, every T-shirt, every pair of underwear.

I open the locker but close it again almost immediately. It feels wrong to spy on another girl's possessions. But it's a stronger feeling than that—like the bed in the dorm, I have no claim to this locker either, which leaves me bereft. It reminds me of when I moved away from home: at first, my parents kept my room just as it had been, almost in memoriam, but after time my things were moved out to the garage so Dad could set up an office, and by then it didn't really feel like home anymore.

I was still living with Mum and Dad when I started my first job, as the assistant editor for a literary magazine. I was twenty-one and had just returned from a month-long holiday with Marina. We had travelled around Vietnam, making our way north from Ho Chi Minh City on the national bus service. It had been a wonderful trip; Marina and I travelled very well together. Almost every day I thought about telling her about the girl in the pub in Collingwood—I hated concealing it from her. But I was scared. I knew Marina thought girls being with girls wasn't proper, that there was something unnatural about it; she'd said as much to me many times before—never in a deliberately cruel or even hateful way, but with a cool, steely certainty.

A few weeks later I spent New Year's Eve with two new friends: a girl named Laura and a boy named Ben. I'd met them the night I first went out in Collingwood and we'd kept in touch in the months since. After drinks at Laura's, we had a meal in South Melbourne, and eventually we made our way to the Stanley.

The pub was full, steam already sneaking around the bottles lining the bar. Dim red lights blinked from each corner. We had more drinks, and danced in the middle of the sweaty dance floor. After a while I excused myself to go to the bathroom.

As I washed my hands a girl strolled in with a small cigar snagged between her teeth. After she'd been to the toilet she joined me at the basin, a fug of smoke hanging about her dark head. We started talking, and outside, on the landing, she asked if she could buy me a drink. We spent the next few hours dancing, and early the next morning I went back to her flat in Brunswick.

I'd never met anyone like Eva. She was quite girly in many ways, slight and almost fragile-looking, but there was also something aggressive about her—in her swagger, in the way she looked at women: openly, with blatant desire. At first I found it shocking, which she sensed and played up to, but after a few dates I think we both grew bored; just as it had been with Fraser, we ran out of things to say.

One night Eva invited me to a gay dance party on Smith Street where I was introduced to some of her friends. I felt shy around them—they were all cool, inner-north types, with tight black jeans and asymmetrical hair. Except for a girl named Cate, who wore a pinafore.

It was dark and loud upstairs. Eva played pool, rounds and rounds of it, hardly speaking a word to me. In fact Cate was the only one who made an effort to talk. It turned out we'd been at Melbourne University at the same time—we had probably shared a seminar.

'Film and Sexuality?'

'Yes!' Cate grinned. 'That essential component of an arts degree.'

When Eva was done playing pool we all went downstairs to the dance floor. By now it was late, almost closing time. All of a sudden the interior lights came on. I remember raising my hand against the glare, and how Cate had stood there, a hand on her hip, sipping at her drink, something so bright red just looking at it made my teeth ache. She turned to face me as if she'd felt me watching. All night she had been hidden in the dark and now I saw her properly for the first time: her fair hair, the dusting of freckles across her nose, her green eyes, dark—almost flinty. I thought she was beautiful.

'She's got a girlfriend, you know,' Eva said later, after we'd said goodbye on the street outside the club. She kicked at a McDonald's wrapper fluttering against a grille.

I didn't see Cate until the next week, at a party in a grotty share house in North Fitzroy. I sought her out, and we talked beneath a tree until her girlfriend came over. She said she was going home—'I'm too drunk'—and Cate's eyes flashed at me in the shadows.

When her girlfriend had left, Cate and I went inside. We had another drink standing at the kitchen sink, then I said I needed to use the bathroom. 'Come with me?' I said. 'Just to make sure no one barges in?'

'Sure,' Cate said, putting down her glass. She followed me down the hall. I didn't use the toilet. In the doorway I took a step towards her, but she edged away, her back hitting the wall. She stared at me, her lip turned up, almost inquisitively, and for an awful moment I wondered if I had misread her—until she kissed me.

~

There were times I felt overwhelmed by love for Cate. I'd never experienced these feelings before: all that longing and all that lust. It was an aching sort of love which, whenever I have tried to trace it back, like trying to find the source of spring water, always takes me to that sticky dance floor, and thinking as those lights went on: *You. I want you.*

Ruby was the first friend I told about Cate. The morning after one of our early dates I met her for breakfast at Mr Tulk near the State Library and explained how I had met this girl and I really liked her.

I never thought Ruby would react badly to this news, but I was still incredibly nervous. But she just put down her cup and grinned. 'So when can I meet her?' she demanded. I was so relieved, so elated, that I was trembling. I don't think I stopped smiling for the rest of breakfast.

It was the same with Liv, the same with Simone: unconditional happiness for me. But I wasn't so lucky with others. When I told Marina over a coffee after work, she raised a hand and said, 'Please, don't feel like you need to give me any details.'

I was so stunned I didn't know what to say, and we sat in silence for a while, gazing out the café's window at the pedestrians on the street. Marina finished her coffee and said, rather primly, that she had to go. I waved her off a few minutes later, feeling sick and humiliated. I almost chased after her, to apologise, but for what?

Over the next few days Marina didn't return my calls or answer my emails or text messages. At first this rejection felt unreal. Friends didn't do this to each other. Friends talked about these kinds of things. I couldn't understand why she was behaving like this. 'What about our future?' I wanted to shout at her. 'What about those bloody sports cars you're always going on about?'

I couldn't sleep with worry. She must be revolted, I kept thinking. She must despise me. As the weeks went on with no contact, it began to feel like a wound, deep and nasty. Marina, it turned out, would never speak to me again.

After this reaction I decided not to say anything to Mum and Dad. I still needed more time to process everything in my own head, and I also wasn't too sure how they would respond—I certainly wasn't expecting the champagne to be popped, but I didn't anticipate open hostility either. My parents were educators; they cared about social issues; Mum voted for the Greens. But one night at the dinner table it just worked its way out of me.

We'd been watching a segment on the news, something to do with gay rights, and a woman had come onscreen talking about her girlfriend. My mother looked at me and crossed her knife and fork. 'She seems very worked up about her *friend*,' she said.

'Her *girlfriend*, Mum,' I said.

'Hmm?'

'Her girlfriend.'

'Why are you being so particular?'

I shrugged. 'Because that's who she is. There's a difference.'

Mum smiled. 'And I suppose you have a girlfriend, do you?'

I could see she wanted to take the words back as soon as they left her mouth. My mother has never been confrontational; it must have been playing on her mind for some time. Where, after all, had I been spending my weekends for so many months? Who was I speaking to on my mobile phone each night, in my bedroom with the door shut?

I set down my cutlery. 'Actually,' I said, 'I do.'

Dad took a large gulp of wine. Mum laughed. Then, gradually understanding that I wasn't joking, she began to pack away the empty plates, stacking the dishwater noisily. The television droned on, until Dad stood up and turned it off.

I stayed at the table, my heart beating hard. Still no one said anything. I had expected it to feel like a relief to say those words, but now I felt squeamish, like I had been caught doing something wrong.

~

A few weeks went by. I hadn't mentioned Cate again, and my parents hadn't asked about her either. Then it was my birthday, and Mum organised a home-cooked dinner to celebrate, inviting Archie's girlfriend over for it. When I asked why Cate hadn't been invited, Mum said, 'But I didn't think you'd want to bring anyone.' A small smile played on her lips. 'What?' she said. 'Have I done something wrong?'

I stared back. Mum has such a soft, kind face. But her eyes had hardened in a way I'd never seen before and for the first time I was afraid.

At dinner I sat across from my brother's girlfriend, made small talk and drank too much. I didn't want to be there, acting as though part of myself—my *real* self—didn't exist. It made me feel sick.

A few days later, I scraped together enough courage to speak about it again with Mum. She was out in the garden, watering the orchids in pots. But she didn't want to talk. 'Not today, please,' she said, turning her back on me.

'Why not?' I said. 'It's important that we discuss this.'

'All right,' she said, putting down the watering can. 'If you really must know I think you're making a huge mistake. Why are you doing this? You've had boyfriends before. Why don't you want a boyfriend? What about Fraser? You liked Fraser, didn't you?'

She was wearing her tortoiseshell sunglasses and her eyes were invisible behind the dark glass. But she was angry, I could tell from the rigid set of her jaw—more angry than I'd seen her in a long time.

I wasn't prepared for this reaction and I felt stunned. 'It's not about having a boyfriend. It's not about a choice,' I said.

'You'll regret it,' she said, shaking her head. 'This is the thanks I get, I suppose.'

'Why don't you listen to me?' I said, crying now. 'Why aren't you trying to understand?'

I thought my tears would worry her, maybe even shame her. But Mum spun around, her bloodless lips drawn across her teeth.

'I don't have to understand it,' she said. 'I'm sorry, that's just the way it is.'

~

Time stretched out, and still no one spoke about Cate—not me, or Mum or Dad. I tried not to worry about it. It was a lot to take in, I reasoned, I shouldn't expect too much, too soon. I'd heard all kinds of stories about parents' reactions to their children's coming out. I'd heard of people being thrown out of home, beaten up, and in some cases taken to the family priest for quasi-exorcisms. I was lucky, in comparison, to have encountered such a muted resistance.

Since it was impossible to talk about it with Mum without causing an argument, it became easier not to talk about it at all. I didn't talk much about my relationship outside the house, either—not to colleagues or old friends or anyone I met outside the safe environment of Cate and our circle of friends.

Eventually I decided to move out. Ruby and I had been talking about it for ages and now seemed the right time. We found a townhouse in Northcote overlooking a gym and an outdoor swimming pool, with parkland behind it. The house wasn't much to look at—red brick with a low concrete fence and a few weeds sprouting from cracks in the front steps—but I loved it.

I loved living with Ruby, too. Most days we worked different hours—me nine to five at the magazine, her part time at a call centre. Ruby was also in a band that was starting to create a buzz. When she wasn't playing, we'd hang out at home, and on warm evenings we threw open the glass doors and drank G&Ts on the balcony. Sometimes her boyfriend, Joe, came over, and when Cate was also staying the four of us had dinner together. It all felt, finally, grown up.

But things weren't going so well between Cate and me. We weren't seeing as much of each other; she blamed this on her new job with a media company. She wasn't happy there: the hours were long and her work repetitive. When we did catch up, she seemed distracted. For the first time we started to argue—real, protracted arguments—and I began to worry about whether our relationship would last.

The townhouse had a third bedroom and Ruby and I needed to find another housemate. Cate knew someone looking for a place. I'd met Alexis once, when she'd joined a bunch of us for drinks after work one evening; one of Cate's friends fancied her. Alexis worked in a boutique in the city and had a boyfriend, though she also liked girls. 'And don't forget she doesn't believe in monogamy,' Cate had said about her, rolling her eyes.

Alexis came over to the house one evening for a glass of wine. She was still dressed in her work clothes. I felt nervous around her. She seemed very glamorous next to me in my tracksuit pants and T-shirt.

'It's a shame, isn't it?' I sighed as Ruby and I sat on the balcony after she'd gone. 'I like it here with just the two of us.'

Ruby smiled. 'Alexis seems cool, though,' she said. 'Don't you think?'

'Mmm.'

'And quite pretty.'

I laughed. 'Yeah, I suppose she is.'

Ruby laughed too. 'Oh yeah?'

I put down my glass, shaking my head. 'Oh no,' I said. 'No way. I wouldn't go there.'

'Well you *do* have a girlfriend.'

I stared at the flickering streetlight. I hadn't seen Cate all week and her absence was starting to agitate me. What was she thinking? Did she miss me? I loved her so much, but I could feel myself drawing further and further away. Sometimes I'd catch myself imagining what it would be like to be with someone else—to kiss them, to sleep with them. Even to love them. How was I going to fix this?

~

Alexis took the room downstairs, next to the lounge. As I parked out the front, I saw the downstairs lights tinted pink against the venetian blinds. Inside the house smelt of vanilla.

Later I found her in the kitchen, dressed in a navy hoodie, cooking on the stove. She offered me some wine and we sat at the dining table.

'To housemates,' I said, raising a toast.

She laughed, clinking my glass. 'You dag.'

It was an easy transition to a house of three. When we were all at home, we cooked together and ate at the dining table, serving up great goblets of wine. But with our similar hours I found myself spending more time in the house with Alexis than with Ruby.

She was easy to be around. Inquisitive, too, asking me all kinds of questions about my work, what I read, what I thought about simple, unexamined things. Often our conversation drifted towards relationships. She liked to ask about Cate. How we met, how we got along. Eventually I told her about the problems we were having and how I felt we were drifting apart.

I expected judgment. But Alexis only nodded, watching me thoughtfully. 'Love is so complicated,' she said. 'Isn't it?'

She'd met her boyfriend, Mike, in a film studies tutorial. He was older and wore suits with skinny black ties. I'd only seen him once at the house, and when I did I thought: *Poor bloke*. He'd come upstairs for a cup of tea and I watched the way he looked at her, with a kind of proud, worn-out longing.

One evening I heard them return late from dinner. It was impossible not to know when Alexis was in the house—her high heels always echoed around the cavernous downstairs living area. I waited in the kitchen, smiling when I heard her exclaim. That afternoon I had found a stray kitten mewling at our front door and while his owner arranged to collect him I'd set up a saucer of milk and tuna in the laundry.

I crept downstairs. Light from the car park glowed at the frosted window. Through the stairs' railing I glimpsed Alexis, dressed in a skirt and a black trench coat, her dark hair spilling down her back. The kitten was coiled happily in her arms. I felt my face flood with unexpected colour. Ruby was right: she was very pretty.

~

A few weeks later we threw a housewarming party. I had been assigned to the kitchen, where I made ginger and lime cocktails and baked bruschetta. Alexis sat on the bench next to the oven, her heels banging against the cupboard. I don't know if it was all the noise or the people, but she seemed nervous, almost skittish. She'd hardly spoken to anyone else, which was strange because most of the guests were her friends.

I drank another cocktail. They were getting stronger. When I asked Alexis if Mike was coming she shook her head. 'We're not together anymore,' she said.

'Oh, I'm sorry to hear that.'

She smiled. 'Are you?'

We watch the others dance on the balcony until I asked if she'd like to look at my bookcase.

'Okay,' she said, smiling again.

I led her to my room and closed the door. Alexis sat on the edge of my bed while I stood next to the books. As I went to pull out the copy of Daphne du Maurier's *Rebecca*, about to explain how I was named after Maximilian's first wife, I felt the swish of her dress against my leg.

I turned around and next we were kissing, stumbling back towards the bed. Alexis laughed, pulling me up, and we kissed again. We were still kissing when Mia, a friend of Cate's, burst into the room.

She stood swaying in the doorway, a half-drunk cocktail in her hand. 'I made a fool of myself in front of Ruby!' she wailed. 'I asked her to sing for me. Can you believe it?'

Mia looked from me to Alexis, hiccupped, and walked out of the room.

'Phew,' I said. 'That was close.'

Alexis raised an eyebrow. 'She saw, Bec,' she said. 'She just didn't say anything.'

Later, when everyone had gone, I tucked Cate up in my bed, kissed her goodnight and went downstairs. In the shadowy lounge, Alexis was curled up on the couch. I sat beside her, and she took my hand and we kissed again. I thought about Cate upstairs and began to cry: great, racking sobs. How could I ever explain to her what had happened?

~

Cate must have sensed something the next morning. 'Is everything okay?' she asked after we'd eaten a fry-up with Ruby and Alexis.

'Mmm,' I said. 'Yeah. Why?'

'You seem a bit out of sorts.' She kissed me on the mouth. 'I love you.'

I despised myself. *What a coward you are*, I kept telling myself. *How weak*. But I just couldn't muster the courage to tell Cate the truth. I didn't want to hurt her, but more than that I didn't want her to hate me. Thinking about confessing sent me into contortions of panic. Lying was so much easier, so much safer. I almost convinced myself that the deceit wasn't real if I didn't speak of it.

One night when Ruby was out I went down to Alexis's room. We sat on her bed for hours, talking about this and that. I still didn't know whether she liked me and I didn't know her well enough to intuit her intentions. Maybe this was all a big game to her?

'You have to break up with Cate,' she said gently. 'So we can be together.'

'You want to be with me?' I asked, hardly believing it.

She smiled and frowned at the same time. 'Of course I do,' she said.

But I never did tell Cate the truth.

Instead, when I sat her down a few nights later, prefacing the awful conversation with 'We need to talk', I told her I felt like we'd grown apart—that maybe we needed a break to know whether we really wanted to be together.

I started crying midway through and Cate asked in a small voice, 'Have you cheated on me? Is that it?'

I looked up, my breath caught in my throat. Here was my opportunity, offered up so generously. But I still reeled from it. 'No,' I cried. 'How could you ask me that?'

Cate found out anyway, a week later. Someone had heard something; the rumour had spread. 'I give it three months,' she seethed, confronting me one night after work. 'See how much you enjoy your polygamous relationship with Alexis then.'

The friendships I'd made through Cate were over in an instant, a year and a half of confidences at parties and dinners and nightclubs destroyed. My group of gay friends was gone forever. Alexis and I were both sent angry text messages and emails, informing us we'd been banished to the wilderness.

'Oh well,' Alexis said, tossing her phone aside. 'Can't really blame them. But don't worry: we'll make new friends.'

But she didn't yet understand that she made friends far more easily than me; she didn't understand how traumatic the demolition of this new and safe world felt.

~

I never forgot about Cate or what I had done. When I look back, I think some of the shame did seep into my new relationship, but in a perverse way it made it seem, from the beginning, much stronger. I still marvelled that Alexis wanted to be with me; she'd been so patient through it all, and as the old bruises began to fade, my feelings for her flourished.

We built a cocoon at home: cooking together, sharing a glass of wine, watching movies from our local video store. On the weekend we slept late, eventually dragging ourselves out of bed to read the paper and maybe go out for brunch. I drove us everywhere on my scooter: down to the beach, to the market, to the village around the corner with the Art Deco cinema and cocktail bar across the tram tracks.

I was very happy. We had a lot of fun together—Alexis made me laugh, mostly at myself. And we talked about everything. I think that is what I fell in love with first: her sharp intelligence, her argumentativeness. Her tastes were indiscriminate, and we often disagreed. When I remarked that Cate and I had hardly argued, Alexis said, 'That's because you didn't love her like you love me.'

And I did feel loved. Alexis made me feel so very safe and secure during those first few months together. She was so confident in who she was and what she wanted. I remember walking down the street with her one morning, only a week or so into our relationship, and she had reached for my hand. I wasn't used to this public affection and I recoiled from it, embarrassed. But she'd grabbed my hand again and held it tightly. 'What's the matter?' she asked. 'I want to hold your hand. I'm proud to be your girlfriend.'

But still that doubt was niggling at me. How long would it be before she grew tired of it being just the two of us? It felt like disaster was always just around the corner, that at any moment Alexis would announce that she was going out somewhere without me, that she was staying over at a friend's. That she would say: *You're not enough*.

There was also new friction at home. Ruby had been subdued at the news of our coupling, but I had promised it wouldn't change anything about the house. But Ruby hadn't been around as much, and was staying over at Joe's more often. 'You don't want me here spoiling the romance,' she once said, smiling faintly. But I knew it was more than that.

After a while I noticed that Alexis and Ruby had stopped talking to one another altogether. If the three of us were in a room, they only communicated with each other through me.

Despite my invitations, Ruby never ate dinner with us at the table or joined us downstairs to watch television. Whenever we rode home on the scooter and saw the light on upstairs, Alexis would clench her legs around me and sigh, 'Great. *Boob* is home.'

It had bothered me that they didn't get along. Ruby, after all, was one of my closest friends. But I laughed with Alexis that night, and the next thing I knew I was rolling my eyes unencouraged, because other things had started to irritate me about living with Ruby, like how she never cleaned, how she didn't drink, how there was always a war over using the ducted heating, and how whenever I wanted the house to ourselves Ruby was always, always there.

Alexis and I planned a holiday away, for some time on our own. We headed to Sri Lanka for two weeks before Christmas, staying in a hut at the top of a hill overlooking a turquoise bay. Every day the sky was huge, the sun blazing through the tropical haze. Small red and yellow and blue boats were beached on the sand, and local children frolicked in the shallows.

It should have been perfect. Except Alexis was distracted, checking Facebook at every internet café, or texting on her phone, which never seemed to stop chiming with some new message. At night she stayed up reading on the porch, only coming to bed when I was asleep. She never kissed me. I tried to ignore the growing panic fluttering in my chest until one afternoon, when we did start to fool around, she sat up and threw her hands to her face.

'I can't,' she said. 'I just can't. I'm sorry.'

I pulled the sheet up around my shoulders. 'Okay,' I said.

We went to dinner. I drank three Bacardi and limes, picking at my grilled barramundi. Alexis sat with a glass of wine, gazing off into the distance.

'I'm sorry,' she said again.

She rarely apologised for anything and I looked up. The restaurant behind her was fuzzy around the edges. She reached across to take my hand.

'I just don't think I can sleep with you until I sleep with someone else,' she said.

I put down my glass, stared at it. The table tilted.

'What?'

She sighed. There was something rigid in the line of her mouth now. 'You know I don't believe in monogamy, Bec,' she said.

The barramundi, the Bacardi—all of it was rising from my stomach, up my throat. I swallowed. 'And you thought it would be a good idea to say all this *now*?'

'I didn't plan it,' she snapped.

We walked back to the hut along the sandy track. Laughter drifted up from the bars lining the beach. I drank more beer from the fridge, and went out to the porch. 'I can't believe you're doing this on my holiday,' I said through gritted teeth. 'How selfish can you be?'

Alexis didn't look up from her book, just said: 'It's my holiday too.'

Eventually I climbed into bed. I should have felt wounded, my heart ripped out. Instead I felt empty, like I would never feel any kind of wholeness again. As I lay there, the fan whirling and sweat gathering behind my knees, Mike popped into my head. *Poor bloke*. I started laughing. It sounded like canned laughter in my ears, on a loop, and I couldn't stop, until Alexis poked her head around the door to ask what *was* so funny?

18
~

It's late. We're all in bed, supposed to be reading. Portia and Sarah's beds are empty. They're out in the boiler room—they've been out there for hours, since prep. It's just the two of them—no Ronnie, or Briohny, who is propped up in bed, scowling over the rest of the dorm.

Finally curiosity gets the better of me and I throw back my doona. In the doorway leading to the side path I hear laughter, Sarah's trilling the loudest.

In the boiler room I'm struck by a flume of warm black smoke billowing from the firewood drum. Flames lick up high into the air, halfway to the ceiling. Dressed in a hoodie Portia stands near the drum, hopping from foot to foot. She's holding a bottle and after taking a glug she wipes her mouth and passes it to Sarah.

'Bec,' she bellows. 'Where have you been?'

I glance at Sarah. Two cigarettes dangle from her mouth. 'Looks like you're having a good time,' I say, swatting at the smoke.

Sarah laughs, thrusting the bottle into the air. 'Good times,' she cries.

'Maybe come back inside?' I peer back around the doorway, down the path. 'Miss Lacey will be up here soon for lights-out.'

Portia rubs her eyes, belching. 'Fair enough.' She covers her hand with a sweater like it's an oven mitt and begins dragging the drum towards the door, sparks spitting everywhere. She manoeuvres it to the edge of the path, where it flickers in the breeze.

I watch as they each reach inside the drum and pull out burning logs. Portia brandishes hers almost ceremonially before arcing to hurl it into the night.

Everyone has now come out to watch, oohing and ahhing at the fireworks. The logs tunnel through the air as if they were low-shooting stars. Portia and Sarah work their way through the drum until only a smouldering interior remains.

'Isn't it pretty,' Sarah murmurs as Portia throws the last log. 'They remind me of fireflies.'

Something in Sarah's voice makes me turn, but she's ducked her head to rub at her eyes. 'Bloody smoke,' she says, though we both know she's been crying.

~

It hasn't stopped raining all week. In class, I gaze morosely out the window at the bleak grey sky. There's a crossie this afternoon; the course will be slippery and pocked with puddles. I don't want to run—I need a nap, half an hour will do, just to get myself warm again. But there's no way of getting out of it. My time card is collected at the finish line, and if it's not logged I'll get a detention.

'What if instead of going down to line-up,' Sarah says as we trudge back to the house after French, 'we wait up near the utility track? The route comes by there, and when the pack runs past we can just join them. Cuts the crossie in half, doesn't it?'

So when everyone else heads down to the library, Sarah and I stay up in the house, making a show of relaxing on our beds. At a quarter past four, we scamper to the utility track, hiding in the bushes until the first girls and boys charge past and we slide down the embankment to join the back of the pack.

We run together for about a kilometre before Sarah stops, lashing out at a stone. 'What's the *point*?' she shouts.

We walk on, not talking. More girls and boys run past, flicking up mud in their wake. The air is as thick as Monsieur Gerrard's beef stew. I try to think of things to say, but nothing comes to mind. The silence isn't so bad, anyway.

At the fork in the track is a wire fence; the beginning of an overgrown path is just visible through the paddock.

Sarah points. 'I wonder where that leads?' she says, taking in the large tree with the overhanging branch and the clusters of swamp heath springing from the verge.

'To the road, I think. See? There's a car.'

We both watch the blur of white move between the trees before it disappears. I continue walking, about to call to Sarah, when I see her reach down to pluck a flower from a tall stem. She's smiling.

~

I wake that night to rustling at the other end of the dorm. It's dark, except for the slivers of moonlight through the windows, and I can just make out Sarah moving down the aisle.

Sometime later the fluorescent lights come on. Miss Lacey stands in the doorway, Mr Connolly at her side. She marches towards Sarah's empty bed and begins rifling through her drawers.

'She's at the nurse,' I say. 'She went after lights-out.'

Miss Lacey starts away from the drawers and moves towards me. 'She is not at the nurse, as you well know, Rebecca. She has run away. A driver phoned, after spotting her near Riverfield.'

I sit up, cold leeching through my insides as I picture Sarah marching along the black and endless road, a lone car creeping along behind her.

'I didn't know . . .'

'Do you honestly expect me to believe that?' Miss Lacey says, clenching and unclenching her fists now, like she wants to hit me.

~

The next morning no one knows what's happened to Sarah. She hadn't come back to bed, and she isn't at breakfast either. 'It's like she's vanished into thin air,' Portia says. Even she sounds worried.

Outside the chapel Miss Lacey draws us aside. 'Sarah is safe,' she announces. 'She was found very early this morning, just past Riverfield, trying to hitch a ride to Melbourne. She's going to spend a few days with her guardians in town before she comes back to school.'

As everyone begins filing inside, exuberant after this good news, Miss Lacey draws me aside. 'Bec,' she murmurs, 'I'm sorry about last night. I was just so worried. Anything could have happened to Sarah . . .' She rests a hand on my shoulder, smiling—a real smile, one of sheer elation. She has such a pretty smile, and I feel the hard part of my insides collapse. I'm so tired of being angry with her.

She peers down at me. 'Can we have a truce?'

I nod my head feebly. I don't have the energy to say no. But there is still something urgent clawing at my insides. I'd thought giving in would feel more like relief.

~

Sarah comes back to school different. Her bad skin has flared up again, dozens of pustules on her cheeks and forehead the size of Tic Tacs. She spends hours in the bathroom, dabbing her face with cotton wool soaked in cleanser. She walks every crossie and long run with grim determination. She never does her prep. Her bedside area is constantly failed; I don't see her put clothes out for the wash.

I wonder if something happened at her guardians'. Or perhaps her parents were mad at her for running away. But when I ask about her time in Melbourne, she just shrugs. 'Smoked a bit,' she says with a lopsided smile.

One night, before bed, I find myself in the bathroom with her and Portia. While I brush my teeth Sarah wipes her face with her cleanser, the grey cotton buds piled beside the tap. No one is talking. Portia, I've noticed, has barely spoken to Sarah since she got back.

'Eww,' Portia suddenly cries, flicking a cotton bud on the floor. 'Don't put those near me. I don't want to catch your *acne*.'

In the mirror, I see Sarah's jaw clench. I put my toothbrush down, edging towards the door, but I also want to stay: there's a frisson in the air—something is about to go down.

'Gross, gross, gross,' Portia sighs. 'Everyone is so gross. It makes me sick.'

Sarah pats her face dry. Then she walks up to Portia and pokes her square in the chest. 'You know what?' she says. 'I hate you.'

Portia shrugs her off, but Sarah pokes again, harder this time. The two girls stand like that, locked in a menacing stare, until Sarah starts screaming.

'I fucking hate you! I fucking hate you! I fucking hate you!'

Portia edges away, but Sarah follows, pinning her between the bench and the wall. Then Sarah is laughing, an awful guffaw, tears streaming down her shiny cheeks. The commotion has brought girls running to the bathroom. 'Oooh,' says Briohny gleefully, starfished in the doorway. 'Lovers' tiff.'

~

I'm still thinking about Sarah and Portia's blow-up on the way back from dinner the following night. Simone and Lou flank me, but neither of them are talking and it's eerily quiet. Fog trails along the ground, and from the road I can see the lights are out in the dorm.

After fixing ourselves mugs of Milo, the three of us huddle together on Simone's bed. Simone had been telling us a story at dinner about a boy she likes and I'm eager for her to continue. It's so cold in the house that our breath comes out in white puffs. Stirring her mug, Simone looks to the window at the end of the aisle and her face freezes.

'*Someone's at the window.*'

I glance at Lou and smirk. 'Good one.' It takes more than that to fool me. Even so, I twist so I'm facing the dark glass. I can't see anything.

But then a bang makes us all scream. I rush to my bedside table, rifling through the top drawer for my pocketknife. I'm not taking any chances—it might be some kind of sex-crazed maniac out there, coming to rape and murder us. We're all facing the door, me with the knife raised like a samurai, when Kendall walks in.

'Oh, thank God!'

Kendall stops at the foot of her bed, frowning. 'What's the matter?'

'We saw a man at the window,' sobs Simone. 'Didn't you see him?'

'No.' Kendall pulls back her covers, about to climb in, but she hesitates. 'Why don't I take a look outside?' she says. 'You guys seem scared.'

'Would you really?'

I follow Kendall to the back door and watch her climb over the concrete partition and make her way into the bush. I can't believe she is brave enough to go out there, that she's doing this for us. Spindly trees, like bad spirits, stoop towards her. 'Be careful,' I murmur.

Simone and Lou are still sitting on the edge of the bed, white-faced, when I return to the dorm. I'm hardly through the doorway before another, louder scream pierces the air. I spin around to face Kendall charging back inside, her face paler than ever, almost translucent. She thrusts a finger towards the window before scrambling under her covers.

It's all too much. I start screaming, 'We're going to die! We're going to die!' Lou cowers on the floor beside her bed and Simone starts thrashing her arms and legs against the mattress like she's having some sort of fit.

We carry on like this for another minute before Kendall throws back the doona with a loud, throaty laugh I've never heard before. 'Your faces,' she wheezes. 'Oh, man. Thank you. That was priceless.'

'What?' I say, pushing the damp hair from my face.

Kendall wipes her eyes. 'There's nothing out there, Bec. You must have imagined it.'

'What—all *three* of us?'

Before I know what I'm doing I leap off the bed and rush towards her. Kendall draws her knees up to her chin. I don't know what to do now, so I grab the bed end and shake it. 'You fucking bitch,' I scream. 'You stupid fucking bitch!'

I stop, sagging over the rail. Kendall stares at me. 'Sorry,' she mumbles.

I rub at my forehead, which has started tingling uncomfortably. 'Not good enough. When I tell the others, you'll fucking well regret that.'

I stagger down the aisle. Simone and Lou have stopped crying, and have their hands raised to their mouths.

~

At first no one believes us about the man. But when they see how shaky we are, they soon grow scared too, and after I've told them about Kendall's trick, Sarah marches over and throws the towels hanging over her bed end on the floor. 'One, two, three,' she shouts, grinding them under her foot. 'You dumb bitch.'

When Miss Lacey comes on duty, I take her to Simone's bed and make her sit where we sat. Next I escort her to the window and we peer into the darkness. 'I've never been so scared in my life,' I breathe against the glass.

She turns to me, pursing her lips. Her eyes drift past me to Simone and Lou, sitting on the edge of their beds, then to the other girls lingering by the door.

'I'm sorry, Bec,' she says. 'I don't think there's anyone out there.'

I blink. 'You don't believe me?'

'It's not that . . .'

'But you don't believe me?'

'Rebecca,' she says, pushing her palms into her eyes, 'I don't know what else to say. There is no one out there. What you saw, if you did see anything at all, was a trick of the light. A shadow or a reflection. But no one is out there.'

'I saw someone!'

Miss Lacey sighs. 'I'm sure you *think* you saw something, but I know from experience that you didn't. The school's boundaries are very well protected.' She leans towards me. 'Anyway, this isn't the first time you've cried wolf about this sort of thing.' She raises her eyebrows and I'm certain a smile twitches on her lips. 'Try to get some rest tonight. You're all very tired. This term is always tough, especially with the cold.'

'Why doesn't she take us seriously?' I mutter after she's gone.

Portia looks up from her sketchpad and scoffs. 'Too busy shagging the assistants.'

'Stupid slut,' I say.

Portia blinks, before throwing back her head to laugh.

~

It is only later, when I've changed into my pyjamas, that I hear voices and the tinny rattle of laughter. I wander through to the bathroom where Portia and Sarah are standing outside a steaming shower cubicle.

A moment later Kendall steps out, wrapped in a white towel, and she eyes the girls as she moves to the sink. Her hair is gathered in an elaborate bun, but a few ringlets have come loose, sticking to her throat like tendrils of blood.

'What are you looking at?' she says to the mirror.

'Just your beauty,' Portia says. 'Your ravishing albino locks.'

They're on either side of her now, and before Kendall can say anything they've yanked the hem of her towel, pulling it clean off.

'Hey!'

But they're gone. Out of the bathroom and through the back door, the towel fluttering like a matador's cape. Kendall runs after them, her feet padding across the tiles. I follow, taking the side path to the front of the house, where I almost trip over naked Kendall crouched on the steps.

'Looking for something?' Portia points towards the drying room. 'Go on. It's in there. We were only having a joke.'

They look away as Kendall scuttles up the steps. But when she is inside the drying room, fumbling around in the dark, Portia rushes at the door and slams it shut.

Sarah starts laughing. 'It isn't even in there.' She points towards the corner of the deck where the towel lies in a wet lump.

Portia struggles to hold the door fast, her feet sliding out from under her, until it suddenly falls still. Then, from deep inside the drying room, comes a sound I've never heard before—the sound I imagine a cow makes when her calf is taken away. Deep and elongated, raw with distress. I can't bear it.

'Let her out,' I plead. 'Let her *out*!'

But Sarah bangs and bangs on the door.

'See how you like that,' she shouts, veins standing out like cords on her throat. 'See how you like that now!'

I stay out on the deck after they've gone. It's as if I'm rooted to the floor. *How has this happened?* I wonder, feeling nauseous. *Why are we like this?* A few tears roll down my cheeks.

Eventually the drying-room door creaks open. Kendall's face is ghastly, blotchy and warped out of shape. I haven't seen her cry before, I realise, which seems extraordinary after everything that has happened.

She doesn't look at me as she scurries over to the corner, her flesh almost scaly under the lights.

'Kends . . .' I begin as she bends over to pick up her towel.

But she is already down the steps, taking the path towards the back door.

~

The next morning Portia decides Red House won't get out of bed for breakfast. 'To protest against Miss Lacey for not believing Bec about the man,' she declares. It has to be all of us, she insists, otherwise it won't work.

I don't object. I feel like I've been thrown under a truck—every part of my body aches and my eyes are puffy from crying. Just before I fall back to sleep, I look across the beds to Kendall, but she is lying on her side, her back to the rest of the dorm.

On her bedside table lies the bottle of Impulse. Last night as we prepared for bed, after Portia and Sarah and the drying room, Kendall had reached for that aerosol and set herself alight. Up and down her legs the blue flames had pulsed, like a giant forked tongue, and as she danced around the top of the aisle, laughing a high-pitched cackle, I thought, with cold dread, *What have we done?*

I flew out of bed and scrambled towards her. But others reached Kendall first, beating her down with their pillows. The flames were extinguished almost immediately, a wisp of black smoke drifting to the ceiling.

When the lights came back on, everyone's faces were fixed in stunned horror.

I was shaking. I couldn't stop. 'Are you out of your fucking mind?' I shouted.

A few beds down, Simone glared at me. 'Kends,' she said, 'are you okay?'

Kendall peered down at her pyjama pants. They were singed, and the smell of the scorched aerosol wafted through the dorm. But when she looked up, she didn't say anything. A faint smile played on her lips. Simone waited, then shrugged and climbed back into bed. But I could see in the reflection of Kendall's pale eyes how she was retreating—back into her dark, silent, secret cave—and now I shudder at the memory of it, wishing I could push it out of my head forever.

The tread of boots from the road is the next thing to wake me.

'What *are* you doing? Don't you know it's breakfast?'

Miss Lacey. No one stirs. I can hear ragged air shooting from her nostrils. She must have run from the dining hall. I push my pillow into my mouth, choking on a nervous laugh.

'Girls,' she says. '*Girls!* Get up this instant.'

Someone giggles, and it sets everyone off, a flurry of laughter engulfing the dorm. Portia springs onto her mattress.

'You can't tell us what to do!'

'It's not a *prison*.' That sounds like Sarah.

Then we're all up on our beds. 'Slut,' someone shouts—Simone, maybe—and then we're all flapping our arms about, a chorus of '*Slut, slut, slut*' beating through the dorm. I'm waiting for Miss Lacey to retaliate, to threaten us with Stonely Roads or Mr Pegg. But there is fear in her eyes—real, tangible fear—as she flattens herself against the doorway, her face crumpling.

When she flees we all cheer like a flock of hungry gulls. I catch sight of a ghoulish yellow face in the window, the mouth caught in a snarl, eyes narrow and steely, and I'm shocked to recognise it as my own.

19
~

I wash my hands in one of the basins in the bathroom and splash icy water on my face. In the mirror I see how circles smudge my eyes, and dark roots have begun to show in my hair. I lean in and check my nose for any spots, having a half-hearted squeeze.

The smell is stronger in here. Mould, but it's damp now, slightly antiseptic. Light filters through the high, dusty window, bouncing off the tiles, and when the wind rattles at the window it makes me jump.

I have always remembered how much power Portia had in the house, but I had forgotten just how effectively she had wielded it. Maybe that was why I hadn't written about any of it in my diary—her unrelenting rule was what had frightened me most. Or maybe it was because I was still trying to comprehend my own complicity in everything that happened up here.

On the bench near the basin are vanilla reeds in a small vase. Their smell fills my nostrils, tickles my throat. The memories of Red House have become jumbled in a way I never expected. Time and people are mixed up, like I have picked at bad stitching and the garment has unravelled. It wasn't supposed to be like this. I was supposed to be in control of this journey, in control of what I remembered and how. But instead of Portia or any other Red House girls, now I have Alexis here in the bathroom with me.

~

Things weren't great after we came back from Sri Lanka. The holiday hadn't felt like a holiday in the end, and almost as soon as we walked in the front door arguments started—day-long brawls about stupid things, like the shopping or what to watch on television.

We were invited to a barbecue at Fran's house on Boxing Day. Fran was a new friend of Alexis. I didn't have a good feeling when we left that morning, but throughout the afternoon Alexis hardly left my side as guests sprawled out on picnic rugs, sharing beers and handing around sizzling-hot meats on paper plates.

In the evening everyone headed out to a club. As soon as I walked inside, Alexis pulled away from me, looping her arm through Fran's. They got a jug of beer from the bar and headed to the courtyard. By the time I'd bought my own drink and went to join them, they'd moved to the dance floor, where Alexis had her hand on Fran's shoulder, laughing riotously at something she'd just said.

My face flushed hot. Suddenly everything in the dingy club felt near and dirty. I went to buy another drink, and came back to find them gone. I spent ages pacing up and down the corridors and around the sticky side rooms, until I found them in the bathroom, pressed together in a toilet cubicle, kissing.

'What are you doing?'

I was shaking with rage as I held open the flimsy door. Fran at least had the decency to fix her eyes on the floor. But Alexis just stared at me, defiant.

I ran out of the club onto the street and hailed a cab. All the way home I heard Cate's jeering voice in my head: *I told you so.*

Back at the house I had a shower. Under the needling water I felt strangely calm. Finally I felt tears building, and I hoped they might also bring on anger or pain, but I was still feeling numb when I dried myself off. After I'd changed into pyjamas I sat out on the deck, which vibrated from the party next door. Had that really just happened?

Alexis didn't come home until early the next morning. I woke to the sound of her key in the lock and her high heels clacking across the floorboards. She didn't emerge from her room until late in the afternoon.

The following day more arguments began. About Fran and respect and love. About what it was to be in a relationship. They were awful arguments, with me shouting and crying until my throat felt raw. But Alexis never cried—she spoke in a quiet, controlled voice.

'How can you do this to me? How can you just humiliate me like that?'

She folded her arms. 'I'm not trying to humiliate you,' she said.

'Don't you even care? Don't you even love me?'

'It's not about love. You knew this was who I am. You knew this when we got together. I've never made any secret of it.'

I shook my head. 'You just don't want to take responsibility for anything.'

That set her off. She started shouting hysterically—telling me to get out of her room, that she couldn't stand the sight of me. That she hated me.

After she'd slammed her door, I stood for a moment on the threshold before shuffling upstairs.

Ruby had come home and heard everything. I smiled sheepishly as I passed her in the kitchen.

'Why do you let her speak to you that way?' She was staring at me in horror, and I felt a new kind of shame blossoming inside me.

That afternoon I rode my scooter down to Westgarth and bought a ticket to the next movie showing at the cinema: *A Single Man*. I bought popcorn and a lemonade, and I sat in an empty row near the front. I cried as the previews rolled, then checked my phone. I had three missed calls from Alexis, along with the message: *Where are you?*

As the film went on, I pondered what it was keeping me there, in that house, with Alexis. I loved her, but I didn't want that kind of relationship. Was it the slivers of tenderness we still shared, that she only reserved for me, the one she loved best? Or was it that look I saw in others' eyes, appraising her, admiring her? We had been through so much just to be together, with Cate and the backlash from her friends. Was it pride, or was it something more complex, to do with fear and loneliness?

I gazed at the screen. Maybe it was none of those things. Maybe it was that I enjoyed what I was feeling now—alone and miserable in the cinema—in a way I couldn't comprehend. Maybe I took pleasure in the humiliation of it. My eyes filled with tears again.

When I got home she was waiting on the couch, her arms crossed.

'Where have you been? I was worried.'

That night we rode to the supermarket. It was late, and the aisles were mostly empty. As I pushed the trolley through the fruit section Alexis threaded her arm through mine, drew me close. 'What's up?' she said.

I examined an apple. 'You know what's up.'

Alexis looked at me, and for a second I thought she was going to get angry again. Instead she brushed her hair out of her eye and sighed. 'You know what the problem is?' she said. 'I want to be single, but I don't want to lose you either.'

I shook my head. 'Well that's just fucking great.'

She was still watching me. Her eyes were bruised-looking. 'I'm only being honest,' she said.

~

Every time Alexis and I went somewhere I felt anxious, scrutinising everyone who came near her, talked to her, touched her; waiting for them to swoop in and steal her from me.

Then, one night, she didn't come home after work. She didn't answer her phone or reply to any of my messages. I lay in bed, my stomach curdling, checking my phone every minute until I wanted to rip my hair out.

Eventually my phone pinged with a message telling me she was staying over at her friend Damien's house. I stared at the blue screen until the words blurred.

When she came home the next day she didn't come upstairs. I heard her moving about in her bedroom, then the shower. At last she came to the kitchen and put on the kettle. I heard her make a cup of tea, bang around for a bit longer, then move across the floor towards my room, knocking softly on the door.

'Yes?'

Perched on the end of the bed, she didn't say anything for a while. Just smoothed my brow and stared at the wall. Eventually she said, in a quiet voice, 'We have to break up. I'm so sorry. I can't see another way.'

'You weren't staying with Damien, were you?'

Alexis shook her head, looking sad. I rolled on my side, facing the wall.

'You were with her, weren't you? With Fran. You slept with her.'

'I don't want to hurt you,' I heard her say.

'Do you want to break up?'

'No,' she said.

'Do you still love me?'

Silence. Then, stroking my hair: 'More than anything.'

I rolled back. Glancing up at me from her tea, Alexis looked, for the first time, scared. She was wearing her hoodie, and her face was white, delicate without make-up. I almost smiled. That's how I always liked her best—unadorned.

'It's fine,' I said. 'I understand the monogamy thing, how it isn't for you. But we don't need to break up.'

I sounded like a robot, a dim part of my brain not believing what I was saying.

'But you don't want this,' she said. 'It's not fair.'

'It's okay.'

'I mean it's not fair on *me*. You don't want this, and I'll just keep hurting you.'

'No you won't,' I said. 'I understand. This is how you are. This is how it has to be.'

Alexis nodded. But she wasn't really looking at me; I could tell her mind had wandered off some place else, far away from my stuffy bedroom. She checked her phone: she had a friend due any moment. They were going to a gig nearby. Did I want to come? she asked as she stood up and smoothed down her sweatpants. As she did I caught her looking at herself in the mirror.

'I don't really feel like going out tonight,' I said.

'I want you to come,' Alexis said, squeezing my hand. 'Please come.'

Eventually I was persuaded, and I promised to meet her there.

When she was gone I roamed around the kitchen like a sleepwalker. I made some pasta and took it out to the balcony overlooking the fluorescent-lit pool, a bottle of cheap wine at my feet. I stared at the bowl of pasta, then put it to one side, reaching for the wine. After I'd popped the cork, I drank straight from the bottle.

It took me ages to walk to the pub. Up a long, dimly lit street, and along the main drag, which was bustling with Saturday night revellers.

The band room was crowded. Alexis bought me a drink, and when the band came on we sat near the front, her arm looped through mine, her friend on the other side. After a while Alexis leant into me and nodded towards the singer. 'She's hot, isn't she?' she said.

When the band finished and the lights came on, a girl came over and asked if she could buy Alexis a drink. Alexis took my hand. 'No, thanks,' she said. 'This is my girlfriend.'

The girl looked me up and down. 'Oh,' she said. 'Sorry.' She melted into the crowd, turning once to give Alexis a sly smile.

Alexis was watching me, frowning. 'Are you okay?' she asked. My hands were shaking.

It was never going to work. What was I thinking? I knew who Alexis was, what she wanted and needed from a partner—and it was never going to come from me.

It was just like Lara, back in primary school, and Portia in Red House. It was a repeating relationship, repeating behaviour. Like I had with them, I hoped that Alexis would change—I *needed* her to change—to prove to everyone, including myself, that this relationship was real; that I hadn't made a mistake, that I hadn't disappointed anyone, that it had all been worth it—all the cruelty, all the humiliation, all my own bad behaviour. I kept thinking about Mum, and how she'd said I'd live to regret the choices I'd made in love. Like anyone has a choice in love.

I went home with Alexis that night. But things didn't go back to how they were before—how could they?—and like an animal backed into a corner, Alexis became more brazen and more cruel. There was a girl she went home with on my birthday, and then one, who she spent a lot of time with in the end, who took her horse riding for a weekend away. 'It was *so* not me,' she said, laughing, when she came home late on Sunday evening. 'Can you picture me, Rebecca, riding along the beach? Argh! What was she *thinking*?'

But I could picture it and I couldn't get it out of my mind.

'It's not cheating,' she later shouted, a vein pulsing furiously on her forehead. 'You agreed to this. You said *yes*. I'm the one who should be angry. *I'm* the one who has been cheated. Tricked. You made me believe you were someone different. You made me believe you're someone you're not.'

When I finally turned around and said *enough*, Alexis let out a sigh and nodded. 'I'll have to go back to Dad's for a while,' she said, looking at me as though she was wondering how we ever could have loved each other, and what should have felt like a relief, like the end of something long and painful, but at least the end, opened up like a black and endless chasm.

~

The sun has launched itself from behind the clouds. Everything flits by—too fast; I feel dizzy. I plunge down the hill, past the chapel, tall and dark and draped in shadow, down the steps near the classrooms. I have to get out of here.

I fling open the car door and scramble inside. I sit with my head pressed against the steering wheel until my heart slows. But my mind is swarming: Emma's shocked face, Portia's laugh, Alexis's back to me. Shame worms its way into my guts. *This* is where it started. Here—at Silver Creek. This is where the fear began. And it was of my own making, not anyone else's.

You're always the victim, Alexis used to complain. But that is how I've always remembered it.

After I start the car, I pull out my phone, meaning to check the map to work out the best way to the campsite. But I can hardly think straight. I'm remembering that night I went to the bar on Smith Street. Alexis had been there, with some other girl, and I stood in the corner and drank. When I walked over and tugged at her sleeve, Alexis had rolled her eyes. 'Bec,' she said, 'I don't want to talk to you right now.'

'But I'm so unhappy,' I moaned. 'How can you not care?'

Her hands flew into the air. 'Because you're impossible! I can't be around you when you're like this.'

Swallowing the last of my vodka raspberry, I'd stormed out with the parting threat of *driving home*. I crossed the road, looking back to see if she was watching. She wasn't, but that didn't stop me getting in the car. I could feel my phone vibrating in my handbag, but I wasn't going to answer it. She couldn't tell me what to do.

I drove past the bar, and took the corner. That would show her, I thought with a smile. That would show her I was in control. Then I saw the red and blue lights in the rear-view mirror, and my heart started banging.

Flicking on the indicator, I glanced at the back seat, hoping I might somehow find someone there. But I was entirely alone.

20

~

Mr Hillman's daughter Libby is back this afternoon. I find her loitering on the deck, red icy-pole smeared around her mouth. She has been visiting the house more regularly, as though lured by some dark power. When I begin rubbing sealant into my hiking boots out on the deck, she trots over to watch, leaning her warm torso against my back. She smells of crayons.

'Go home,' Sarah snaps from the drive. 'You're not allowed up here. We'll get in trouble.'

But Libby doesn't listen. She climbs on top of the barred-metal washing crate. It's empty today—we've just had laundry.

When Portia comes outside and spots Libby, I can almost see the cogs turning.

'Do you like that crate, Libby?' she asks.

Libby nods emphatically. 'It's my favourite.'

'Would you like to climb inside?'

Portia hoists Libby into the air, at the same time tipping open the crate's lid with her knee. Libby peers inside, hesitates. Her blue eyes flicker in my direction.

'Maybe—' I begin.

But before I can say anything more Portia has placed her inside. 'You have to crouch,' says Portia, pushing on Libby's dark head. 'So you can fit. See?'

Again Libby hesitates. Her mouth hangs open, her big bottom lip trembling. But I can't tell if she is afraid when she squeals and drops to all fours. Portia slams the lid and snaps on the padlock. She looks at Sarah and they both fall about laughing, and I am laughing too because Libby has squished her face against the bars. Portia grabs her camera and takes a few snaps. 'Kids are so weird,' she sighs.

Kendall appears in the doorway. 'You shouldn't do that,' she says.

'What?' Portia juts her chin.

Kendall so rarely speaks out that we've all turned and stared.

'Libby shouldn't be in that crate.'

'She likes it in there—look.'

Libby clings to the wire. She is shaking all over, like a dog left out during a storm. I glance back at Kendall. She is watching me with her head cocked, and doubt begins unspooling deep in my stomach.

I can't stand her judging me—of all people, it seems worst coming from *her*. But then a voice comes floating up from the road, and leaning over the banister I see Miss Lacey heading towards the house with Mr Hillman.

'Quick,' Portia says. 'Get that calico.' She crouches beside the cage. 'Hey, Libby, if you're *really* quiet when I put this over your crate—and I mean silent as a mouse—we'll have a surprise for you. You like surprises, don't you? Do you like chocolate?'

Libby sniffs, peering through her filthy fingers.

I can hear Miss Lacey and Mr Hillman in the dorm. We have only a few seconds before they'll walk through to the deck. If they catch us with Libby, I don't know how we'll ever talk our way out of this.

Portia throws the calico over the crate. Libby flinches, banging her head against the metal lid.

'Maybe we should just let her out?' I croak.

'She's fine,' says Sarah.

'Is she?'

'Oh, make up your bloody mind, Bec,' Portia snaps.

We're sitting along the length of the banister when they fill the doorway. Miss Lacey narrows her eyes; she knows us well enough to know we never loiter innocently on the deck like this.

'Girls.' Mr Hillman smiles. 'Have you seen Libby about at all?'

He is standing just a few paces from the washing crate.

'No, I'm sorry,' Portia says politely. 'Is she all right?'

'Oh, I'm sure she's fine.'

I say nothing, staring at Mr Hillman's skinny legs. They're covered in dark, fuzzy hair. He always wears stubbies, even in winter. A drip of sweat runs down my back.

When they've gone, Portia throws back the calico. 'That was close,' she breathes.

It takes some coaxing, but Libby eventually raises her head. She grips my outstretched hand, bringing one leg out, then the other, and then takes off, down the steps and along the road. She didn't even want her reward.

There's a small puddle of pink liquid on the crate's floor. 'I think she's thrown up,' I say.

Portia puts an arm around my shoulder and chuckles. 'Kids are disgusting, aren't they?'

~

I can't stop thinking about Libby and her frightened face pressed against the bars of the crate. I wish I had walked away, joined Kendall. Her judgment weighs uncomfortably, like she's seen some private part of me that I never wanted to expose, and I avoid her around the house. But I watch Portia closely. I have a horrible feeling she's got something else planned.

When I come back after class the next day, I immediately sense something has happened. I don't know what it is, but girls are dotted around the dorm, their faces taut. I find Briohny near the fireplace. Ronnie stands beside her, chewing at her nails.

I dump my books on my desk. 'What's going on?'

Ronnie looks at Briohny, who nods. 'Drying room,' Ronnie breathes. 'Go and see it for yourself.'

The drying room is empty except for suitcases and storage crates. The door is already ajar. Suitcases are stacked around the small room. The heat is on and the room pongs, condensation at the glass near the roof. There's a large blue suitcase in the middle, with a yellow nametag bright against the tiles. *Kendall.*

Ronnie comes to the doorway, her silhouette long across the floor. I take a step further into the room and sink to my knees. I reach out, fearful of this object, and run my hand over the cracked leather casing. It is cold, despite the warmth of the room. Taking a deep breath, I flick the catch and raise the lid.

In the middle of the suitcase, like an ancient offering, is a giant human turd. The room fills with a wet and meaty stench and I reel from it, gagging, and slam the lid shut. I scramble for the door, for the fresh air. Ronnie moves aside to let me past.

'Who did this?'

I follow her to the deck, but she won't answer me—just shoves her hands in her pockets.

'Ronnie, who *did* this?'

'Sarah,' she hisses. 'It was Sarah, okay? Fuck.'

'What? *Why?*'

She shrugs. 'Portia told her to do it.'

I feel lightheaded. I dangle a hand against the banister, the first ripple of understanding breaking through me: how we'll all be implicated in this, every last girl in Red House.

'Does Kendall know?'

Ronnie leans out, surveying the road. In the fading afternoon light she doesn't look beautiful anymore, only washed out, bloodshot. 'Not yet,' she says.

~

I don't bother searching for Sarah. She'll be up in the bush, perched on an overturned log, smoking. It's Portia I want.

I find her on the edge of her bed, flicking through a magazine. 'Before you say anything, it wasn't me,' she yawns. 'It was Sarah.'

'But you told her to do it.'

Portia looks up, frowns. She's wearing a cap and her hair sticks out like straw. 'Can't change what's happened now.'

'Do you know how much trouble you'll be in?'

'Me?' she says. 'Are you deaf? It was Sarah.'

When she turns to a new page I snatch the magazine away. 'What is *wrong* with you?'

She's on her feet in a flash, shoving me in the chest. I lose my balance, dropping the magazine.

'Who the fuck are you to tell me what to do?' she growls. '*Sarah* did a shit in the suitcase, not me. It was a joke, a dare. I never thought she'd actually do it.'

She picks up the magazine, rolls it up like a baton and begins slapping it against her leg. *Slap, slap, slap.* I watch her, transfixed, my resolve disappearing like the air from a punctured balloon.

'What has Kendall ever done to you?'

Portia's brow creases. She peers down, into her lap, where she's tightened her grip on the rolled-up magazine. Then she looks me straight in the eye. 'Nothing,' she says. 'Nothing at all.'

~

News of the 'shit in the suitcase' spreads around the school like wildfire. As Red House files into the dining hall, someone sneers, 'Feral bitches,' and when lunch is served a roll is chucked at our table, clattering onto Emma's plate. None of the teachers do anything about it. I wonder where Miss Lacey has gone.

'Everyone knows,' I groan. 'The whole bloody school. We'll never live this down.'

'What are you so worried about?' Briohny says. 'You didn't do it.'

Finally Miss Lacey appears. Her face is paler than usual, but her throat is covered in a rash, which seems to be spreading from her chest. Sarah, she tells us, has been expelled. 'She's up at the house now, packing her things.'

Miss Lacey toys with a fork at the end of the table, her face unreadable now.

'You're not to go up there, girls,' she says through gritted teeth. 'You're to stay away from the house.'

I expect a protest but no one says anything. Don't they care? Despite what's happened, I hate to think of Sarah up there on her own, so when the meal ends I slip out of the dining hall and run back up the hill.

But when I walk back into the house I find the dorm empty. In the far corner Sarah's bed has been stripped bare, the drawers hanging open.

'Sarah?'

She is gone. I slump against the empty cupboard, my feet sliding out from under me. The tiles are cold on my legs. I hang my head between my knees and let out a strangled sob.

When I hear a sound of boots across the floor, I look up to find Kendall standing in the doorway. She takes a few steps inside, walking around in a small circle. Her face hangs sadly.

'I had to,' she says. 'I know everyone will hate me more for it, but . . .' She worries at her crimson bottom lip. 'It was just too much.'

I get to my feet. I feel woozy, my own sweat sour in my nostrils. 'I know,' I say. 'Everyone knows it. And . . .' I swallow. 'I'm sorry.'

She tries to smile but her lip just trembles. She seems so much older, prematurely aged, and I think: *We did that.*

~

Emma and I sit on the balcony. It is cold tonight. We should be in bed but the assistants have left us alone. Everything is different now that Sarah is gone. Briohny, who had slept next to her, has already repositioned her bed to give herself twice the room, her mattress now facing out over the dorm like a throne.

'You didn't wait long,' I'd muttered from across the aisle.

Briohny only laughed. 'Just making the best of a bad situation.'

Down the hill, Yellow House's lights flash through the dorm and a burst of shrill laughter travels across the dark. The air smells of fire, of burnt wood, of ashes.

'Maybe things will be better now,' I murmur.

Emma says nothing, leaning over to pick at a scab on her knee. It's a big scab, covering most of the kneecap, and I watch until the sensor light goes out. But we don't move. We just go on sitting there, the moonlight drifting in and out of the clouds, sliding through the night like a blade.

PART FOUR

21
~

I get into Cattlemans Flat just as the cold starts to seep up from the ground, pulling into an empty spot about thirty metres from the river. The rush of fresh water, the overturned gum in the middle of the campsite, the pit toilet discreetly nestled behind a few trees—it's all the same.

Other campers are scattered around the grassy site, some of them listening to the second half of the football on the radio. The couple across the road wave; they have an enormous fluffy white dog sitting at their feet.

Before setting up, I head down to the river, which is high after the recent rain. Light threads through the trees. Perched on a rock, I watch the fast-moving current. The water is brown and black and jade, and all around the bank are rocks, some white and bare, others jagged and grey, covered in moss. A leaf flutters to the sleek surface and is whisked along the rapids until it disappears around the bend. Near the bridge a large branch, trapped under the stones, protrudes from the water, shuddering in the passing current.

I wonder what Mary would make of my visit to Silver Creek. A few months after I was caught drink-driving, I decided to make an appointment with a counsellor. I wasn't coping; I felt like I had fallen into a bad place and I couldn't find my way out. I wasn't sleeping, and I wasn't eating properly, either. I would sit down to a meal, almost delirious with hunger, only for the food to make my stomach turn. I would have to force it down, fighting the urge to retch. I'd lost fifteen kilograms in three months.

More than this, I was worried about how the conviction hadn't changed that much about my behaviour. I was still going out several times a week, drinking heavily—so much, in fact, that in the morning I couldn't remember huge parts of the night before. I was becoming forgetful at work, making mistakes; sometimes I couldn't drag myself out of bed at all and called in sick instead. I needed a circuit breaker.

Mary practised from home, quite near to me. Her consultation room, at the front of her house, was a pleasant one, ideal for talking, with a large mahogany shelf filled with books, the kind you'd expect to see in such rooms—a battered copy of *The Second Sex*, a *Companion to Australian Literature*, lots on Freud.

Mary was not a counsellor, I discovered during our first session, but a psychotherapist. 'Lacanian,' she said, glancing towards the reclining couch in the corner.

When she asked why I had come to see her, I sat fidgeting in the chair. 'Well,' I said, clearing my throat, 'I guess it's because I'm unhappy.'

'Yes?'

'About . . . a range of things, really. I was caught drink-driving. And I broke up with someone recently. A girl, I mean.

Alexis. It wasn't an easy relationship. She wanted us to be non-monogamous, actually, which I didn't really want . . .'

'Oh,' said Mary.

I swallowed thickly. 'And then, I suppose, it's other things too. Which are linked to the relationship. Or maybe not. I don't know.'

I'd begun to cry and Mary handed me a box of tissues, ones scented with eucalyptus. I took a few gratefully.

'What other things?' she asked.

I pushed the back of my head into the chair. My scalp was aching from my tight bun. Far away I could hear crying. A baby, it sounded like, in one of the houses on the narrow street, or perhaps a cat.

'I've fallen out with a few close friends,' I said. 'Girls I thought I'd be friends with always. It's been . . . hurtful. I don't know why it has happened.'

I could have been talking about any of my old friends, but I was thinking about Ruby. After Alexis moved out I had grown to despise the townhouse: the tinny hammer of rain on the roof, how it shuddered in the wind. Whenever I woke in the middle of the night I still found myself listening for the sound of Alexis's key in the lock.

Her bedroom sat empty, a thin layer of dust coating the floor. We needed a new housemate, to fill the space and cover the rent. But I didn't want anyone else in there.

Ruby always seemed bewildered by my grief. She may not have liked Alexis, but I still wanted her to comfort me: to take me out for a meal or a glass of wine. I wanted to talk to her about Alexis—and apologise and begin to make amends. But we never spoke of it; our friendship had frayed so much that only a few threads were holding it together.

I started looking at other share houses. After a couple of weeks of interviews, I was invited to move into a terrace in North Fitzroy. All I needed to do was tell Ruby.

By then we were barely talking. But it was more than that—something had hardened in me. If she didn't care for me, why should I be bothered with her? As the days stretched on, I could feel myself retreating further from the announcement.

The week before I was due to move out, when I knew Ruby would be at work, I began to pack up. I didn't have many things—Alexis had taken most of the shared furniture with her.

Ruby came home that evening. As she glanced at the piles outside my bedroom I finally confessed that I was moving out.

Ruby chewed at the edge of her lip. 'When?'

'This weekend. But don't worry! I'll pay up the full month of rent.'

'You're leaving this weekend and you're only telling me *now*?'

I took a step back. Ruby never raised her voice, and her face was puckered with rage.

'You haven't been around,' I said.

'I haven't been *anywhere*!'

Only then did it occur to me that she might care about me leaving. But I didn't have the chance to say anything else because she had already stormed into her bedroom and slammed the door. She left again a few minutes later, taking an overnight bag.

Lying there on Mary's couch I had swiped a tear from the corner of my eye. I missed Ruby. I hadn't seen her since I'd moved out months ago. Sometimes my imagination strayed to a scene where I ran into her, which was always unsettling. Not because I was afraid of what she might do or say—I liked to think she would be friendly and polite—but I knew, just *knew*, that I'd turn and walk in the other direction, avoiding the confrontation.

I told Mary all of this, and cried some more. When I stopped I played with the tissue, rolling it up like a cigarette.

'And I'm just so sick of myself,' I moaned. 'I mean, a friend suggested I volunteer for something—like a soup kitchen—so I could help other people and stop being so sad and thinking about being sad. But,' I wailed, 'I couldn't even do *that*!'

Mary listened to all this impassively. She scribbled a few notes in a notebook. I liked that—her aloofness. Mary dressed well, wearing a pinafore, black stockings, expensive shoes. I wondered how old she was—fifty-five, maybe. Her eyes were sharp and very blue, and she spoke in a distracted, faltering sort of way.

'And what about Alexis—are you still in contact with her?'

'No,' I said. 'Sort of. Well, yes.'

'How?'

'We talk on the phone. Send text messages now and then. Sometimes I miss her. But I don't want to. I'd like to be free of her.'

'Free?'

'I don't like her,' I said. 'I don't like who I am when I'm around her. I feel alien in my own body.'

'But you still keep in contact with her.'

'I know—it's ridiculous. I can't help it. And each time we communicate I feel worse.'

Mary seemed to think about that for a while. Then said: 'You're still in love with her.'

I hung my head. She was right. But that was how it was back then. How I thought love went: the measure of it. Every kind: friends and family, especially lovers. The good with the bad, like honey laced with poison.

Mary scribbled in her notebook.

22

~

These holidays are different. I don't go out much and I don't see anyone—no friends, and no other family. I only leave the house to trudge down to the video shop, where I borrow *Aladdin* and *The Lion King*. I must look deranged with my unbrushed hair and dark circles under my eyes; I catch the lady behind the counter eyeing me suspiciously.

Nan isn't staying with us anymore. She lives in a nursing home now. She still isn't herself, Mum explains as she prepares dinner my first night home. Mum also looks tired—it's been a long term for her too, with teaching and reports, and visits to Nan after work. I chew on a ragged fingernail, drawing away a chip on the tip of my tongue. I feel guilty about it, but I'm glad to have my bedroom back.

The next day we visit Nan. It takes her a few minutes to recognise us. Her clothes and hair are scruffy, and her eyes roam about the ceiling like she is following something moving up there. A tiny Italian lady sitting nearby starts babbling at Archie before leaning over to give him a slobbery kiss on the cheek.

'What is actually wrong with Nan?' I ask on our way home.

Mum glances out the window, her brow creased. Traffic streams by. 'She hasn't had an easy life,' she finally says. 'Always looking after everyone but herself.'

When we visit a few days later Nan is dressed more neatly in a blouse and skirt. She's chatty, too, asking me all sorts of questions about Silver Creek and crossies and schoolwork. She smiles her cheeky smile, her gold filling winking, and for some reason I want to cry.

'That was nice, wasn't it?' says Mum on the drive back through the city. She taps the steering wheel, humming a tune under her breath. She asks us what we'd like for dinner, and when I say fish and chips she agrees, just like that, putting her hand over the seat for Archie to squeeze. I lean my head against the cool glass, watching houses flit by.

~

I sit up in bed, my heart thudding. The phone has been ringing through the dark for ages now—why isn't anyone answering it? Eventually I make out Dad calling to Mum. I don't hear anything after that until a sob echoes along the narrow hallway.

It's Nan—I know it—and I clench the edges of my doona, tears already pooling in my eyes. I picture Mum cradling the phone, alone in the cold kitchen, and I begin howling into my pillow.

Dad pads across the hallway and knocks on my door. He's wearing an old grey T-shirt with a rip at the neck. His face is pinched, a deep furrow in his brow, just as it gets when he's furious about something. He sits on the edge of my bed in silence for a few moments, then reaches for my hand. 'Poor Mum,' he murmurs. 'Poor Nan.' Then he leaves the room, closing the door behind him, and I hear him move across the hall to check on Archie in the next room.

I fall asleep again around dawn. When I first open my eyes to the rose-patterned wallpaper I have a few moments of calm forgetfulness before it all comes flooding back.

I stagger into the hallway. My eyes feel swollen and my lips are dry. There's a comforting smell of coffee and toast coming from the kitchen. Mum is sitting at the bench in her pink dressing gown, and I give her a half-hug. Her face is sticky. She flips through some household bills before big tears begin falling from her eyes.

A bunch of roses arrives from Mum's best friend. When she finds the card among the stems she begins sobbing. Dad comes to her side and rubs her back.

'I just . . .' she says. 'I just . . .'

'Shh,' says Dad.

I stare into my bowl, my own miserable tears welling in my eyes. I long to go to her, to comfort her and make her happy again. But I don't know what to say, or how to make this better.

~

A week later, I'm sitting with Simone on the bus back to Silver Creek, listening to her stories about her holiday, where she stayed with her dad and went to the football a few times.

I don't tell her about Nan.

By the end of the first week, I still haven't told anyone. I don't know why I keep it a secret. I could talk to Simone or Emma about it; I would get upset, but that would be okay, they would be kind. And that's what you do, don't you, when someone you love dies? You talk about it.

I feel like I've betrayed Nan by my silence. That I am taking her apart, piece by piece. That I am *unremembering* her. I can't stop thinking about the funeral, how my cousin cried in the row behind me but I didn't: not one tear. I had wanted to be strong for Mum, who sat at my side, wiping her nose from time to time, stuffing pilly tissues back up her sleeve. I wish I'd cried like my cousin. I wish my family had witnessed my grief and not my stony self-control.

After the service we stood on the verge outside the church. I didn't know what would happen next: I'd never been to a funeral before. I expected we'd all go somewhere to talk, and the kids would be fed. It was a nice day, sun and blue sky. Only as the black hearse pulled away did Archie start to cry, throwing himself against Mum, tearing at her dark blouse, stabbing a finger towards the vehicle rolling down the road. No one knew where to look.

Lying in bed in the dorm, I scrunch my eyes at the moonlight. I wonder where Nan has gone. Where is she buried? We didn't follow her to the cemetery. This is all I can think about.

The next morning I sit at my desk with my diary open and mark the date when Nan died with a green cross. And in the weeks that follow, I'll turn to this page, remembering not that she's died but all the wonderful memories I have of her, and I reflect on the comfort of this cross, its endurance, its intractability, however private, however silent.

~

The days are getting longer and warmer. In the morning I find light at my window, even some blue in the wide sky. Birds start to gather in branches outside the house, singing long, shrill tunes into the afternoon. Around campus, flowers are starting to push through callused buds. That smell is everywhere—rich, sweet and slightly sickly. It is the smell of change. And the Final Hike is only a few weeks away.

I have teamed up with Simone and Lou in a hike group, along with Ruby, a girl from Yellow House. She is tall and willowy, with a deep, husky voice.

I feel safe with these girls. It is an odd feeling, this safety. If I am quiet and thoughtful, they leave me alone. I can make bad jokes and they still laugh. While the hikes get longer and harder, and my body adapts to the recurring pain in my hips and the niggles in my knees, other warm feelings start to bloom in the dark cracks inside me. For the first time I imagine life after Silver Creek, down at the Big School next year. I won't have to start all over again like I did here—I will have friends. There is so much to look forward to.

Since coming back from the holidays I've stayed out of Portia's way. In fact I've hardly spoken to her since Sarah left. Hours can go by without me thinking about her, and seeing her sprawled naked across the bed I wonder how I could have ever sought her good opinion.

Then something wonderful happens. Portia, Ronnie and Briohny sign up for the school athletics carnival, which means they're going away for a whole week. Each year students from Silver Creek can travel down to the senior school for training and the interschool competition at Olympic Park, in Melbourne. I would have signed up too, for the triple jump and the hurdles, but not this time. The last place on earth I want to be is stuck with those three in a poky dormitory.

The next morning I watch them march down the road on their way to the buses. *Seven days*, I say over and over in my head, like a mantra. I'm still standing there, squinting out the window, long after they've disappeared. I expect them to come charging back, shouting, 'Surprise!' But the minutes stretch to hours and my chest expands like I'm breathing properly for the first time.

~

The rest of the week goes quickly. Nothing is different, of course—there are still crossies to run, prep to finish, jobs to do. But their absence is exhilarating.

Midweek there is another long run in the chilly afternoon. The sky turns grey and puffy, with a few bursts of rain. The course is fifteen kilometres, climbing and descending about half-a-dozen jagged knolls. But as I stretch out my hamstrings at the starting line I feel a surge of confidence. *You have to keep running the whole race*, I tell myself. *You can slow to snail pace, but you're not to stop.*

The gun fires, scattering the pack. I take off fast, moving towards the front. In among the low-lying trees the air is moist, tickling the back of my throat. My lungs soon start to burn.

On a steeper incline the wind picks up, buffeting the back of my legs. Everything seems to be moving in slow motion, my feet weighed down like dumbbells, my arms leaden and aching. I can hardly breathe; my throat burns.

The wind is howling now, throwing up leaves and sharp bits of bark. Grit stings in my eye.

Finally I reach the top of another knoll. A blast of icy wind makes my T-shirt billow. My knees buckle as the gradient changes, and I almost fall. But I keep tottering down the hill, sliding in mud. I'm nearly home.

When I cross the finish line someone thrusts a time card in my hand, and a place. *Fourth.* I stare at the tag, hardly believing it. I stagger around the car park, sucking in great gasps of air. *Fourth!*

Miss Lacey jogs over and gives me a hug. 'Well done, Bec!' She is beaming.

More staff and students congratulate me. It *is* a great effort, I keep telling myself. I've made it into the top ten—and I didn't stop, not once. I can't wait to tell Dad, and later, at dinner, when the results are announced, Red House all cheer when my name is announced. 'Rebecca Starford,' Mr Bishop says. 'Dark horse there in fourth place.'

~

After dinner, I flop on my bed and stare at a spidery crack running from the cornice. I'm exhausted, but it is a tranquil exhaustion. My mind is clear.

Rolling onto my side, I glance about the dorm at the girls preparing for bed. Around the table tonight there had been no great rush for the cordial, or snatching of the condiments before they were shared around. Now, after showers and supper, we're all reading quietly in bed before lights-out.

Out in the tuck room, I find Simone and Emma sitting up on the bench. Each has her hands cupped around a mug of tea.

'Hey, jock.' Simone grins.

I grab a Roll-Up from my locker and lean against the bench. 'Tonight's been nice, hasn't it?' I say. 'Shows that we actually *can* get on as a house. Maybe we should . . . I don't know . . . all stand up to Portia a bit more? You know, stick together.'

Simone nods. 'Sure,' she says. 'We could try.'

Emma stares at the tip of her moccasin. After a long sip of tea, she says, 'No offence, hon, because you know I love you, right, but you've been up Portia's arse most of this year.'

I fidget with the sticky wrapper, feeling my cheeks burn. 'I know. But I don't really want to be like that anymore.'

'So what do you suggest?' says Emma. 'Because I know if we make pacts, the moment those girls walk through the door it will go back to how it was before. She has too much power—had it from the very first day. It's too hard to change that now.'

I don't know how to answer that, but when I feel a hand on my shoulder I look up into Emma's freckled face.

'It's okay, you know,' she says. 'Everything that's happened: it's okay. You don't need to take it all on your own shoulders.'

~

The next afternoon they're back, lounging around the dorm, and disappointment weighs on my chest. But then I remind myself about how great everything had been while they were away—how for the first time it felt like there was real harmony in Red House—and I feel a little brighter. When Portia traipses in after her shower and begins to tap talcum powder to her pubic hair, I think: Why should we all be afraid of her? It's ludicrous. So as she starts loudly recounting a story about Rollo Walker that we've all heard a dozen times, I sit up and shout, 'Can you please shut up? Some of us are trying to read.'

The dorm goes quiet. I lay back, my heart squirming. No one has ever told Portia to shut up.

She smiles thinly as she surveys the dorm. 'What have you been plotting while I've been away?' she says. 'A revolt?'

She laughs, a long, horrible cackle that makes my skin crawl. She keeps talking, louder now. I don't say anything, and neither does anyone else. Maybe Emma was right.

~

Simone and I huddle together on the deck. Her hair is wet from the shower and she leans against the banister, shivering.

'I don't have a good feeling about this,' she says, peering into the dark. 'It's like in Greek myths, where the hero challenges the gods and is struck down for it.'

I raise my eyebrows. 'That's a bit dramatic, isn't it?'

Simone's eyes shine under the lamplight. 'I'm just saying. You can never plan how things turn out.'

23

~

The following weekend we have the Sawmill/Pict hike, four days covering nearly one hundred and twenty kilometres. It's notoriously difficult. We'll need to get up at dawn in order to scale each mountain in daylight. But I've heard the views from the summits are extraordinary, stretching all the way to the ocean.

I can feel these longer hikes all through my body. In my joints, grinding as I sit down at the table for formal dinner; in my feet, tender inside my school shoes; in the back of my legs, tight like the skin on a drum.

The first day of the hike is sweltering, but I hardly notice: Simone has us all laughing so hard at a story about her brothers that we have to ditch our packs to catch our breath. We hike on, the sun burning our necks and forearms. By Queen River we stop for lunch and I wash my feet in the shallows. Afterwards

Lou and I wander further downstream and find smooth pebbles that we skim along the surface.

We arrive late into Mag's Hut, the sun already dipping behind the distant hills. I hardly have strength to put up the tent.

We've only brought two tents, to save on weight, and Simone and Lou squeeze in with me. I haven't brushed my teeth or washed my face. I haven't even changed out of my clothes, and the tent soon stinks of our musty gear. I sleep breathing through my mouth, my nose pressed against the cool canvas. The rocks beneath the floor dig into my back.

It feels like I've only just closed my eyes when I hear Ruby's plaintive wake-up call. Simone grunts, rolls over, her face almost touching mine. There's black gunk in her eyes. On the other side Lou is still fast asleep.

'Guys?'

Simone's eyes flutter. 'If she doesn't shut the fuck up . . .' Her breath is sour.

'Guys?'

I'm so tired I feel queasy. I check my watch: it's 6 am.

Outside the tent, Ruby is boiling tea in the billy, humming a sweet tune. 'Here,' she says, handing me a mug as I stumble out from beneath the fly. 'This will make you feel better.'

It's another long day. The path to Oatland Spur is steep and mostly narrow. The ground is also loose in places and midway up a clump of earth comes away from the track and I fall over. The full weight of my pack brings me down face-first and I graze my knees and the fleshy part of my palms, which sting for the rest of the hike.

The ground is sturdier further up the spur. While the others stop for a drink, I kick my way through the shrubs to a lookout. From this height you can see as far as Mount Kellet, its silken shadows running down the spiky ridge. It's like something out of a dark fairy tale, and I stand out on the bare rock until the girls' calls summon me back to the track.

At the campsite, Simone and I struggle with the tent lining. A few yards away, Ruby is setting up with calm efficiency. When she's done she brings out her patchwork toilet bag and wanders off towards the stream. 'I'll get the fire going before it gets dark,' she calls.

'I swear she's never been to the toilet on a hike,' Simone mutters. We both watch after her until she disappears into some bushes.

'Do you reckon?'

'It's not natural.'

I laugh. Simone looks at me, then laughs too.

'Neither is what comes out of you,' I say.

~

By noon the next day we have reached the saddle of the Pict. It's quiet here, the only sound the faint trill of insects living in the undergrowth. Hanging from a gum's gangly branch is a logbook. We're the first girls' group in.

After a quick lunch we leave our packs beneath the trees. Part way up, the track disappears and a new path cuts through a dark, narrow tunnel.

Back in the open air Ruby leads us towards another track, over more concealed roots and wobbly rocks covered in yellow moss. When I put my hand out I'm shocked at the soft, warm feel of them, almost like flesh.

Finally we reach the summit, sparse except for a few clusters of trees and shrubs. There's no wind up here either, just a bleached-looking sun off in the corner of the sky.

I tramp over to a ledge, getting down on my knees to sprawl across the ground, peeking at the scene below. How small the people are, clustered around the packs. Trees, puffy like dull green cauliflower, blot the adjacent fields, with patches of baked brown earth in between. The sky stretches out past the trees, to the ocean—I'm sure I can almost see it.

What an exquisitely beautiful place we live in. I sit back, suddenly teary, overwhelmed by this mountain and this dishevelled land. I never expected this—this *love*. I take a deep breath, the crisp, clean air filling my lungs, and it feels like I'm also washing away all the grit and sweat and dust.

Several hours later we reach the top of the Sawmill. The air has turned cool and the nearby ranges have been cast in long shadows. While the others wander off for photographs, Simone and I find the last bit of orange sun thrown against a chair-shaped boulder. 'I don't think I can ever get up,' Simone groans, legs stretched out in a V.

'Problem is,' I say, 'we're always biting off more than we can chew.'

Simone's head lolls in my direction, her eyes still closed. 'This coming from the girl with the sausage-and-bread record.'

~

That night we build a fire and cook up a feast. Beef stir-fry, fried salami, Alfredo pasta from the packet. Ruby makes a batch of pancakes with lemon and sugar, singing to herself over the pan. After we've eaten, Lou and I boil a billy of cocoa. At about eight o'clock the temperature plummets and we all huddle around the fire.

'So,' says Ruby, stirring her mug. 'I guess we should think about the Final.'

'Fark,' says Simone. 'Do we have to?'

'Why don't we have a crack at the Circuit?' I mumble through another mouthful of salami and cheese. I haven't stopped eating all evening.

'Dunno. Two hundred and fifty kilometres?' Simone whistles.

I stare into the orange flames. At the start of the year, the Circuit was an insurmountable challenge, but it isn't so daunting anymore—not after today, and not with my group.

'It's a bloody long way,' I say, dusting my hands clean. 'But I think we can do it. We're a fit group, don't you think? We've been training enough for it.'

I'm aware of my voice getting louder, but I don't care. I want to rally them, so we can do this together, as friends. I want to share this memory with them.

'Imagine how good it would feel to finish the Circuit,' Lou muses, grinning.

I glance at Ruby, who blinks excitedly.

Simone leans forward to pierce a marshmallow with a stick. 'Well,' she says, 'that's settled then.'

~

Back at school classes grind on. Exams are only a few weeks away. Girls are starting to panic about them, but I'm feeling pretty good—my grades are improving and I've been doing a lot of preparation. I'm feeling confident, for the first time in a long time.

One night before lights-out, Portia saunters out to the deck with a can of Guinness. A few of us have congregated there after supper. It's a warm night and mosquitoes buzz around our heads.

These past few days Portia has started saving a seat for me at lunch. Yesterday she even invited me to run the crossie with her. I'd made an excuse, and she'd nodded graciously, but today she's kept me a seat at breakfast and dinner. I wonder what she wants.

'You know,' she says, taking a swig of beer and handing it to me, 'the teachers have loads of booze in their houses.'

I take a small sip of the Guinness and grimace. It's too yeasty, shooting right up my nose.

'You know Miss Constantine's away this week?' Briohny says. 'On her house rafting trip.'

Portia strokes her chin, smiling. 'Is that right?'

~

Portia was right. There were dozens of bottles in Miss Constantine's kitchen—beer, red and white wine, vodka, bourbon, gin. Portia took six bottles of wine and beer and hid them near the big overturned tree off the utility track. 'For later,' she says, her eyes crinkling.

Class is about to start, but we're still in the tuck room. Portia opens a packet of Saladas. 'It's not stealing,' she says. 'Her door isn't even locked.'

Emma leans in the doorway, books piled in her arms. 'She's going to know,' she says.

'Who?'

'Miss Constantine, you idiot! She's going to notice her stuff is gone.'

'And what's she going to do about it?' Portia bites down on a biscuit, butter smearing against her lip. 'Trust me: no one saw us. No one is ever going to think it was Red House.'

Over the next three days more girls sneak down to the house. It seems Miss Constantine really does have an endless supply—enough for almost half our house to steal.

'We have such a big stash now,' Briohny gushes. 'After the Final Hike, we're having a massive party. Inviting the boys. You know: Rollo and Ed and Tommo.'

'Your boyfriends, Briohny?' I tease. We're back in the tuck room. Portia hovers in the corner, by the toaster.

'You can only come if you bring something,' Briohny snaps.

I smile. 'But I thought you had loads?'

'You can't have it both ways, Bec. You either bring something, or stay Miss Goody-Two-Shoes.'

I watch Portia scrape strawberry jam all the way to the edge of her toast. She chews—once, twice—then swallows.

'Won't be the same if you're not there.'

When she says this I feel my face flush red. A party with the boys would be a lot of fun. To have my own stash of booze like the others. Then I think of Dad and how I promised to be good. That I *must* be good. Is breaking into Miss Constantine's house really worth it? It's only two weeks until the end of the year.

I can sense Portia watching me. The others have raided the house several times already. Surely, if we all got caught, they'd get in more trouble than me.

'I'm going once more,' Briohny says, her back to me at the sink. 'You can come with me, if you like.'

~

We wait until after lunch, when everyone else is still gathered out the front of the dining hall. Through the trees I glimpse the house, a brown hut with a flat roof flecked with bird shit. I jump at a rustle in the bracken, but it's only a skink, scurrying towards a hollowed-out tree.

'Relax,' Briohny says. 'No one is watching us. Look, why don't you stand here on lookout. Cough really loud if you see anyone. Can you do that?'

'Maybe I should go back?'

Briohny snorts. 'If that's what you want. No one's making you do this, you know.' She stalks away.

I hover beneath a tree, scanning the area. There's no one around, of course. The only movement is the faint rustle of leaves, and far away I can just make out the drone of the ride-on mower. I count to ten to calm the roaring blood inside my head then, to distract myself, I try to imagine the holidays—the beach and the salty heat, and going to the milk bar for hot chips and Coke—but it's all hazy, out of focus.

Then Briohny is back, bottles tucked under her arm. She waves me over, and we push our way through the bushes towards the overturned tree. 'There,' she says, covering the wine with handfuls of dried-out leaves. 'That wasn't so bad, was it?'

~

A few days go by. There are classes, crossies and meals. Nobody says anything about the missing booze. Still, I avoid Miss Lacey as much as possible, certain she will see something in my face that will give me away. I don't see Miss Constantine at all. Maybe Portia was right. Maybe it really was a foolproof plan.

The next morning at chapel Mr Pegg stands at the altar. It's Father Wilson's spot, and from my seat in the front row I can see how ashen his face is, and my heart starts to thud.

'I have a grave announcement to make,' he begins, voice booming around the cloisters. 'Over the past few days a series of extraordinary thefts have taken place on this campus. Someone, or a group of individuals, has systemically broken into a member of staff's private lodgings and stolen large quantities of alcohol.

'I'm asking those responsible to own up immediately. If the culprits fail to turn themselves in, I will have no choice but to call in the police, and this will become a most serious criminal investigation.'

Outside the chapel a noisy mass of students congregates after the service. I push through the sweaty bodies, spotting Briohny beneath the trees. 'What are we going to do?' she wails.

I grab her clammy hands, somehow calm. 'Let's go back to the house,' I say. 'We can't talk about it here, in front of everyone.'

But she shrugs me off. 'No!'

I grit my teeth. 'What do you mean, *no*?'

She edges away, stumbling in the gravel. Her hair frizzes wildly from her ponytail and her eyes are shiny. 'I'm telling him,' she shrieks suddenly. 'I'm going down there right now and I'm telling Mr Pegg what happened. I'm telling him about you, Bec . . . It's not fair if you get away with it. It's not *fair*!'

People are staring. Through the crowd I glimpse Miss Lacey standing near the wall, a hand raised to her throat.

'Briohny,' I say, 'think about what you're doing.'

But she isn't listening. She has already taken off down the hill, her bottom quivering with each violent stride. I watch her for a moment, then trudge back up towards the house.

The crowd around the chapel is dispersing. Briohny is now just a blur of pink and blue. I stop at the top of the path. There's a honeyeater on a branch, and for a moment our eyes meet as I bite on the inside of my lip until the flesh gives.

24

When the air starts to feel heavy I head back to the campsite and hunt around for wood. But everything is damp, or too hollow, and thrashing around in the long grass, dressed in my leather boots and Paddington coat, I feel more like an amateur than ever.

Eventually I gather enough kindling to build a skeleton of a fire, which I fill out with pieces of newspaper from the boot of my car. But I can't get the flames to take—the paper just smoulders beneath the bark and sticks—and I slump back in the foldup chair, smoke stinging my eyes. Everyone else's fires are roaring and I curse myself for thinking I could just return to the bush and morph into some kind of Ernest Hemingway, fly-fishing for dinner and wrestling bears.

I'm about to put out the smouldering mess when the man from the nearby site approaches, his enormous dog trotting along beside him. He's holding out some firelights and proper wood.

'Here,' he says, 'thought you might need these.'

'Thank you so much,' I say, almost weak with gratitude. He nods, glancing from the car and back to me. I wonder if he thinks it strange, me camping out on my own.

When the fire is roaring nicely I make a strong brew of tea in the billy. I grab my bag from the back seat of the car and pull out the wad of letters my family sent me while I was away at Silver Creek.

The first letter is from Archie. He writes in an oddly formal way, proudly announcing that this is the first thing he has ever written on a computer.

The next letters are from Dad. They've mostly been written on his school letterhead. It's fatherly correspondence, full of news about how Australia played in the cricket and what work he's doing in the backyard. At the end of one he writes: *I think about you a lot and wonder how you are going. A few staff say I am more grumpy with you away . . . Still missing you and I still think you're the greatest.*

I read through more of Dad's letters until I come to the last one, from September:

> *I know there have been some difficult times but I am very proud of you and have great confidence in you, your character and your strength. Please know you will always have my love and support in everything you do, and everything you want to do.*

I take a sip of tea. It's gone cold, but I drink it anyway, trying to push down the thick feeling in my chest. Though the light is getting bad, I still reach for the next wad of letters, this time from Mum. I feel nervous, all of a sudden. I have no memory of these letters: what feelings they might describe, what news. I had wanted to find clues in them, like pieces of a puzzle. Now I'm not sure if I want to read them.

Like Dad, Mum writes about the week at home and at work. Her letters are breezy, almost jolly: updates on Archie, news from the street; in particular, our next-door neighbours whose surround-sound television system kept her and Dad awake until all hours. She asks about Red House, concerned about me not liking Miss Lacey—*She's doing her best you know, darling*. She always signs off with love, with a postscript about how she misses me. In one of the final letters she tells me how much she is looking forward to me coming home at the end of the year.

I read this page twice and start to cry. I sit like this for about half an hour, my throat raw, my eyes smarting from the smoke. I feel wretched, but also comforted by finally letting some of these feelings out. I have been worried about this moment all day—alone, camping by the river, reading over these letters. I was worried about what they might unleash in me.

These days I catch up with Dad and Archie regularly, but I can't remember the last time I saw Mum. We don't really talk much anymore. I suppose we are estranged, and I cringe at the word, the shadowiness of it. Though she knows where I live—she could call me or drop by the house if she wanted to. She just doesn't, and neither do I, and now time and the wordlessness hidden inside it has stretched out so far it feels almost impossible to cross.

I draw out another envelope. The address is inscribed in my hand. I pull out a single sheet of floral writing paper and it takes me a few moments to recognise it's the letter I wrote to myself on the night of the Solo camp-out.

Dear Rebecca,

Well, you are a year older and hopefully wiser after the great Silver Creek year. I hope you also found it the best year of your life.

At the moment, I love school and schoolwork, hiking and running. I love the boys and most of the girls. Our House is the best.

We are also known as the naughtiest house in the school. We have had the first hayshed, Stonely Roads, kitchen det, first girls in tents, maybe first Queen Rivers. So we are pretty naughty. So far we've done the first Bell Run of the year, first dorm raid, first yelling abuse at teachers and many other things.

But another look at Silver Creek. My personal side of it. I think it is something I must capture and enjoy the most I can. Sure, there are ups and downs, but I can't afford to lose time over it. It is only one year. Already it is nearly a quarter over and it feels like I've just started here. It's scary . . . When I first came to Silver Creek I felt a little under pressure to enjoy the year because of what Mum & Dad have put into it. But I know I will love it so much and I hope Mum and especially Dad will be glad I came.

I'll stop now. Leave the rest of my thoughts until I read this in a year's time. I love Silver Creek. In a year's time, I hope I still do.

Love,
Rebecca Louise Starford (Red 12)

Folding the letter over, I start laughing, desperate to hug my fourteen-year-old self. Did I honestly believe I might be able to trick myself, reading this letter at the end of the year? Did I really think that if I recorded these thoughts they might overwrite the other unpleasant experiences?

Isn't Rebecca good? That's what parents always used to say, year in, year out. It was true: I had always been a studious and well-behaved child. And after everything that happened at Silver Creek I worked tirelessly in senior school and got excellent grades, believing I needed to make it up to Mum and Dad. I won a place at a top university. I was even offered my first job before I graduated.

But it all seems irrelevant whenever I think back to that dinner when I told my parents about Cate. Because I can see that it was then that my relationship with Mum started wearing away, like water against a rock. It was then that I began to believe that my sexuality had eradicated every good thing from the past and every good thing that was to come in the future, that I had disappointed them, beyond repair. And it has taken me a long time to understand how complicit I have been in this shame.

When I broke up with Alexis, I really wanted to talk to Mum about it. For her to understand that I was in pain; that I was crumbling. But one night, as I cried at the dinner table, she had simply stood in the kitchen and said, 'I hope you don't expect me to be unhappy about this?'

That, I think, was the hardest thing to hear. To understand that I would have to carry this grief around with me on my own. I stopped going to the house for a long time after that, and that impacted on my relationships with Dad and Archie. But I still felt it, from afar: Mum's denial growing harder, calcifying.

It's exhausting, always trying to fix this unfixable thing. There may well come a day when I throw my hands up and say, *Enough*, but not yet. It's still there, the resilience, and I smile, remembering that Outdoor Education lesson. I did manage to take it away with me, after all.

The trees shudder in a sudden breeze. It's getting cold now, really icy. I wipe my eyes. It's now too dark to read anything more. I tuck the letter back inside the envelope. Then I sit back and stare at the fire.

I don't want to lie anymore. I don't want to live a half-life. I don't want to keep carrying this shame around, like a dead weight. *How is anyone ever going to love you*, Alexis once said, *when you don't love yourself?* She was right about that: I want to be proud of myself and who I have become, and to do that I have to let go of some of the past.

And what about Mum? I still miss her, of course—sometimes I can feel her absence, like an ache inside of me. But lately, whenever I think what I would say if she did pick up the phone and call me, my mind always goes blank.

Maybe we need more time. That's what my friends say. I'm not so sure. Now, whenever I picture my mother, I see her all those years ago, when I was a child. I think of her kind face and warm hands, and the certainty of her love. I want her to call me—part of me will always want that—only now I'm not sure what it is I want from her and whether I need it anymore.

25

~

'Rebecca, Rebecca, Rebecca . . . Why do I get the feeling you're only here because you've been found out?'

Sitting behind the large desk, Mr Pegg has his hands clasped around the back of his head. In the corner, Miss Lacey leans against the windowsill, the sleeves of her polar fleece pushed up to her elbows. It is so very quiet in the office; even the birds outside in the trees are still.

'I was going to come,' I mumble, gazing into my lap.

I sense his eyes boring into me. 'But Briohny came forward straight away. Why didn't you?'

I look up. *Because I'm not a vindictive cow.* 'Because I was scared,' I say.

Mr Pegg leans forward, his elbows clunking against the desk. 'The fact remains that you were an accessory.'

The air around me feels suddenly feels viscous. 'I was just

going along for a look,' I mumble. 'I know it was wrong, I really do. I just . . . I don't know . . . wasn't thinking of the consequences.'

'Something you've struggled with all year, wouldn't you say?'

Mr Pegg swivels his chair to face the window. There isn't much to see—just the blur of trees—and he swivels back around.

'I'm going to suspend you for four days,' he says. 'But you'll serve the suspension internally, sleeping in a tent outside the dining hall. This also means you'll miss half of the Final Hike, though you can rejoin your group at the end of the third day.'

It isn't a surprise, but when the sentence is delivered I sag in the chair as if I've been winded. Tears pool in my eyes. *Please, not the Final. Please, not after everything—all that sweat and agony—don't take that away from me.*

'Think yourself lucky,' Mr Pegg, says almost gently. 'The others are suspended for a whole week.' He lets out a loud sigh. 'I'm going to call your father now. Something tells me that'll be worse than missing the hike.'

~

Outside the office the sun shines in the wide blue sky and the air smells of freshly cut grass. It's the exact smell I remember from the morning I left home with Mum.

Miss Lacey follows me out onto the verandah. I scramble down the steps and cross the road, hoping that she'll get the hint that I don't feel like talking.

'Hey,' she calls.

I keep walking, ignoring her repeated calls. But she lunges from behind, pulling me into a fierce hug. A sound makes its way out of my mouth—half a cry, half a snort—and I try to pull away, struggling against all the shame and anger that is bubbling up in my throat. But I soon give in, wrapping arms around her waist. She is all skin and bone beneath her polar fleece.

'I'm sorry,' I say. 'It was a mistake.'

Miss Lacey pushes me away, as roughly as she held me. 'Breaking into someone's house isn't just a mistake,' she says. 'You do understand that, right?'

I nod miserably.

She brings her hands to her face and sighs. 'Do you know how lucky you are, Bec, to have these opportunities? I just hope you can learn from this. That you can change your behaviour and become a better, more honest person. Otherwise you're going to grow up to be an adult no one likes very much.' She tilts her head, scrutinising me just as she had the first afternoon in the dorm. 'I'm not saying this to be cruel, you know.'

Long shadows stretch across the road. Miss Lacey kicks at a piece of quartz and it skittles to the verge. 'What a way to end the year,' she murmurs.

I wipe my eyes with my sleeve. Miss Lacey is no longer looking at me but somewhere far off. There are lines around her mouth. She doesn't seem so youthful now, as her shoulders slump forward and the gravel grinds beneath her heavy tread. And I wish, with sudden, powerful intensity, that this year could have been different; that we could have been friends after all. But it's too late now, too much has gone wrong, and I have been too callous, too thoughtless, even though buried beneath all these hard feelings is something far more complicated, something much like love.

~

Simone sits on the front steps, banging her hiking boots together, dried mud showering from them like snow. Outer tents and blue japaras hang over the banister. The drying room door has been flung open for the first time since Sarah left, while pegged to the washing line sleeping bags and mats air in the warm breeze.

I slump on the end of my bed. There's a curious energy in the house, cautious and constrained, like it was pulsing beneath the floorboards. So it has come to this, I think bitterly: watching on, uselessly, as everyone else prepares for the Final Hike.

In the corner of the dorm Briohny clutches her teddy bear, sobbing. A few beds down, Portia is folding clothes into a bag—to take home, I suppose, on her suspension.

'Do you think you could shut up?' she snaps.

'Don't blame me for this,' Briohny wails. 'We would have been caught anyway.'

Portia shakes her head. 'You stupid bitch, he was *never* going to call the police!'

'But he said . . .'

'It was a threat! To flush us out. And you fell for it.'

Portia tosses a T-shirt on the floor. Her eyes are red and I wonder if she has been crying too. It never crossed my mind that the Final might have meant as much to her as it does to me.

'Do you honestly think the school would call the police and risk it getting in the papers?' she says.

Briohny cries some more. When she's done she stares vacantly across the dorm. 'My dad is going to kill me,' she says. 'I mean *really* kill me.'

'All our parents are going to kill us,' Portia mutters.

'I never thought he'd make us miss the hike.'

'Well,' says Portia, glancing towards me, 'not all of us are. Remind me, Bec: how exactly did you manage to only get an internal?'

Such a question, pitched to trap me, might have rattled me before. But I'm not afraid anymore, not of Portia or Briohny or their power in the house.

'I didn't go inside,' I say. 'I stood on lookout—ask Briohny if you don't believe me. I was still an accessory . . . Well, that's what Mr Pegg called me.'

'God,' Briohny sniffs. 'You'd think we'd gone *Reservoir Dogs* on them.'

She lies back across her bed, running a hand through her hair, which needs a wash. After a while she pulls out her tuck box and rummages around for some beef jerky, ripping open the packet and stuffing strips of it into her mouth.

~

I hear the rest of the school leave for the Final. I don't get up for early breakfast to say goodbye to my group, or wish them luck. I know I should, but I can't bring myself to leave my tent, which has grown hot and soupy as the sun peeked through the wisps of fairy-floss cloud.

Hunger eventually drives me outside and I'm surprised to find another girl waiting out the front of the dining hall. Her name is Amy, and she's from Orange House: it turns out she had also joined Portia and Briohny on an excursion to Miss Constantine's.

We spend the day washing the fleet of Jeeps. Amy doesn't say much. It is hot again and we are both sweating hard by mid-morning. I wear a wide-brimmed hat, but Amy's head is bare; I can already see the first bloom of burn on her scalp. After lunch she complains to Mr Connolly, the assistant supervising us, that she isn't feeling well and asks if she can go to the nurse.

'Sure,' he says, and we don't see her again until dinner.

The next day's task is rock collecting. Mr Connolly drives us down to the front paddock, which is pimpled with boulders and stones. 'You need to take those rocks and put them in there,' he says, pointing to a rusty trailer under a gum.

Most of the rocks are around the size of an overstuffed hiking pack. It takes both of us to lift them.

Mr Connolly allows us a break in the afternoon. I stand by the fence, a hand raised against the sun, staring across the paddock.

A faint breeze whistles up from the road. Far off I can see a couple of trucks and a car.

Amy joins me, chewing on a piece of grass. 'How are we ever going to move all these rocks?' she breathes. 'It's like Monty Python.'

I nod, rubbing at the base of my spine. I don't tell her I haven't seen Monty Python.

Mr Connolly raises his Akubra, fanning away a fly. It's almost pleasant, standing there like that, watching the road.

~

Mr Connolly drives me out to the Circuit's halfway point at Mount Bleak. It's still the afternoon and no one's in yet. After I've set up my tent I go for a walk to the lookout, finding a seat on a boulder that feels like sandpaper against my bare legs. But I position myself in a patch of sun and it's lovely up here, gazing down to the shadows that stretch the length of the valley like witches' spindly fingers.

Day soon tips into night and birds flock across the sky. The girls still haven't arrived, so I decide to make them dinner as a surprise after their long day.

As the sun disappears behind the trees I finally see their silhouettes moving towards the campsite. Simone's long, skinny legs; Lou's strong, slender frame; Ruby's height above them all—and I feel a pang of regret that I have missed the last three days with them. Spotting me they squeal, charging along the stretch of track to pull me into a sweaty group hug.

While they unpack, I shove the jaffle irons in the fire and go for off for a wee. I swat through bush until I'm far from the campsite. But as I pull down my shorts my torch wavers and goes out. Thrown into darkness, I flail for a few minutes, panic rising, until I hear Simone's laugh, then make out a sliver of flame against the starless night.

Crouched in the tickly grass, I begin to cry—tears of relief, this time, that I am back with my friends. At last I can see it: that Portia was never a true friend to me—and she never can be.

~

The next day we hike to Mount Farrier, then on to Farrier Lake. After lunch we head out to the waterfalls, and I have a wash in the basin. Back at camp I cook dinner again—tonight it's beef stir-fry, with packet carbonara pasta. 'I could get used to you getting suspended,' Simone says with a grin.

We pack up early the next morning before another climb of Oatland Spur. Then it's on towards Craig's Hut near the summit of Mount Franklin. It's the longest day of the Circuit. We won't arrive at the site before nightfall.

There had been a celebration planned for this final night of the hike. As much as you can, anyway, with our supplies—some lemonade and sweets brought from our tuck lockers. But as the cold clear night rustles at the alpine peppers, everyone grows solemn. While I make hot chocolate, Simone brings out the packet of marshmallows and begins roasting a few on a twig.

'Can't believe we'll be going home so soon,' I murmur. 'Back to civilisation.'

'Home,' Lou murmurs, leaning her head against Simone.

I wonder what Lou will take back to the farm, what memories will burn brightest. I know I'll take home all kinds of things, many of them unpleasant, many I'll wish I could forget, but I know there will be many good things too, and right now I want to remember this moment most, sitting around the fire; this happiness with my friends.

'Bec!' Lou shouts, pointing. My marshmallow has blackened, sizzling in the flames. 'It's like a melted face.' Lou giggles, tugging at her eyelids. 'Mwwaahhh!'

Simone edges away. 'I tell you what, Lou. You are dead-set the weirdest girl I know.'

We all laugh, our voices loud, and I pick off the burnt skin and place the warm flesh in my mouth.

~

The next morning I stagger out of the tent, rubbing at my eyes. I feel woozy from not enough sleep. But the air is already warm and the cool dew on the grass is glinting like thousands of tiny jewels.

Reaching Clay Hill by mid-morning, and after a quick snack of bread and cheese, we begin clambering down East Ridge. Far off, beyond the trees, I can make out the khaki-green roof of the Silver Creek dining hall. So close. But we're not going back to school—not yet. We have to climb Mount Silver Creek one last time.

The Saddle is empty. So tranquil, too—there's something almost monastic in the cool air. In the distance I hear the trill of birds, calling soft yet clear, and below that, like a bass track, comes an insect-like buzz of smaller birds hidden somewhere in the trees.

We move slowly up the muddy track. How different this is from the first time I scaled the mountain with the rest of Red House. I'd been so quiet that day, so afraid of everyone—afraid of what I didn't know about them, and afraid of them not knowing me. Now, after a whole year living together, it seems we know everything about each other, but that could change in a heartbeat; it feels like we're on the cusp of something momentous and out of our control.

When we reach the top, the sun saunters off behind the clouds, leaving the air strangely sticky. The summit is also empty.

It's eerie being up here on our own, like we're the last people alive. Lou offers to take a photograph and we gather under the gnarled old snow gum, arms around one another's waists, smiles stretching wide.

26

~

Everything happens quickly now. We have to vacate the house. Pack our clothes, empty our lockers, clean the dorm and the bathrooms. Remove all traces of our existence. Wipe it all away. 'We can't have your dirt here for next year's girls,' Miss Lacey says, almost cheerfully.

Floors are mopped, walls scrubbed, windows buffed spotless. I crouch in one of the toilet cubicles and write in black texta on the underside of the ledge, *Bec was here*, with the date. You can only see it from sitting on the toilet, which gives me an odd sense of pleasure. It seems important, somehow, that I leave my mark. That I am remembered.

The bins are already overflowing—with food, books, and so many clothes. Some girls are even throwing away their hiking gear. 'I won't need it again, will I?' Briohny says, tossing her thermals into a black garbage bag. But I'm taking it all home—it cost thousands of dollars.

Somewhere in there are exams, as well as end-of-year games. One afternoon is Quest, a series of inter-house competitions: wheelbarrow racing and Paarlauf relays. Emma and I enter the custard competition and come third.

More entertainment follows after dinner. Each house performs a song, and Red House decides to dress as country bumpkins with chequered shirts and riding boots, though for some reason Portia paints her face with brown shoe polish. We stand in front of the school and sing a variation on 'Give Me a Home Among the Gumtrees':

Give me a drink with the assistants
We can't resist it
A drink or two in the SMQ
A Bundy out the front
Miss Lacey out the back
And she's knocking on Conno's door . . .

The final line provokes a roar around the dining hall and Miss Lacey hides her face behind Mr Connolly. 'Thanks very much, ladies,' she says later, laughing, as we get ready for bed. 'I don't think I'll forget that one in a while.'

~

The marathon is two days away. It hardly seems real as we're each given a commemorative white T-shirt with *Silver Creek* written on the back at breakfast. Mine is so big it fits over my sweater. After chapel I wander down the road, calling out to Ruby to sign my back.

Pretty soon everyone is having her T-shirt signed. We move on to another house, then down the hill. Nestled in the trees is the last girls' house, Jade. Already a few girls have come out with black markers.

'What are you girls doing?'

It's Miss Constantine, marching towards us.

'You're out of bounds,' she says. 'Impinging on the grass. I'll have to report this.'

She points to the ground. Briohny and I each have one foot on the road, one on Jade House's front lawn.

'But we're not doing anything wrong.'

Miss Constantine's eyes narrow. 'You just don't get it, do you, Rebecca? It's not a matter of right and wrong, it's about obeying the rules.'

'Please,' Briohny says. 'We'll get Stonely Roads and the marathon is the day after tomorrow.'

Miss Constantine smirks. 'It'll be a nice warm-up for you then, won't it?'

~

I sit in the shade on the library steps. Beneath the window the plants are wilting. I lick my lips, tasting the salty, cracked skin. 'It must be nearly forty degrees,' I sigh.

Briohny raises her face to me, squinting in the bright light. She's wearing a blue headband that makes her face taut, like a ballerina's. The wind flutters and her gaze shifts off towards the smudge of trees on the hill.

'Like they care,' she mutters.

A Jeep rolls into the car park and Miss Constantine climbs out, a cap pulled over her hair. Spotting us, she raises a hand to the peak. 'Ready?' she calls.

We set off. The air is even hotter further down the drive, burning at my lungs. Sweat pours from my brow into my eyes.

Briohny trails behind me. Once or twice I hear her falter. When she draws up at the cattle grille, Miss Constantine slams on the horn. 'Don't you dare stop!' she shouts.

'Come on,' I call to Briohny, slowing down so I'm at her side.

Briohny jolts along, eyes ahead. I glance at my watch: thirty minutes. It will be tight. I run over the bridge, the creek burbling below me. Over my shoulder I see Briohny trip and careen towards the bank, flinging herself straight into the water.

'Briohny!'

I rush towards her, sliding down the slope and sloshing through the creek.

'I don't care,' she screams, thrashing about in the shallows. 'I don't care anymore!'

'You have to get up. You have to keep going.'

I grab the back of her singlet and haul her towards the bank. She's gone limp like a rag doll, feet dragging over the pebbles, but I manage to get her out of the water. She rolls onto her back.

'No! No! No! I've ruined my Final, I might as well ruin the marathon too.' She's writhing around in the long grass. 'I've ruined everything,' she wails. 'The whole year—and this is how I will remember it. I hate it—I hate it all. I hate the house, I hate being punished all the time. And I fucking hate *myself*!'

I peer over the ditch. I can't see Miss Constantine. 'Please,' I say, climbing to my feet. 'Let me help you. Before she gets back. We can't let her beat us. Come on, take my hand.'

Briohny blinks at me, a smudge of dirt on her nose. She looks so wretched, and I feel a pang of sorrow for her as she reaches out, the first look of gratitude I've ever seen shift across her face.

~

Outside the library Miss Constantine leans against the bonnet of the Jeep. She taps her watch. 'Oh dear, girls,' she calls. 'Seven minutes over.'

As I hear these words my legs give out beneath me and I slump to my knees, barely aware of the sharp stones. What is she going to do to us?

'Oh for goodness' sake, will you just leave them alone?'

My eyes fly open. Miss Lacey storms down the steps, pointing at Miss Constantine. She touches my shoulder on her way past, but it is Briohny she wants; Briohny, whose grey, unfriendly eyes are glazed with abject fury.

But before Miss Lacey can say anything, Briohny has turned her back. 'I'm fine,' she says, and begins sloshing up the steps, her tread grim but also possessing a calm resignation. Miss Lacey watches after her, rubbing at her forehead, then turns to me, eyebrows raised, as though I might have some kind of answer. But I'm staring at Briohny's liquid footsteps already disappearing in the afternoon heat.

~

I wake the next morning with pain shredding my head. My legs feel bruised and a blister swells on my big toe. I bandage it up, and gulp down a few Panadeine Forte before staggering down to breakfast. By 8 am the whole school has gathered in the car park for the start of the marathon.

Whenever I used to imagine the marathon—in the years before I came to Silver Creek—I had always pictured triumph. Not victory, but a sense of achievement, of validation. The year's hard work—all that sweat and tears and pain rolled into one race.

But pressed between two girls in the line-up, wearing my bike shorts and white T-shirt, I feel no excitement, no anticipation or pride, and that emptiness makes me want to weep. I had been looking forward to this moment for so long, but after yesterday's Stonely Road my feet are like bricks and my back is stiff and knotted. How am I going to race thirty-two kilometres like this? I glance around at the other girls—all fresh-faced, stretching in the shade, and drawing great mouthfuls of water from aluminium bottles—and my shoulders slump. That small reserve of energy I had tucked away for today, those final drips of juice, is gone.

After the gun goes off, I find myself somewhere near the front, though girls and boys soon run past me—hundreds, it seems, until I'm sure I'm in last place. I can't move easily; everything feels tight, clunky, and I have no will to push through it.

It takes me nearly five hours. I run for most of it, stopping to walk when my side burns with a stitch, or when I feel burpy after the drinks stop. On and on the race goes, until I'm sure I'll never finish, sure my body will give up on me and I'll need to be helicoptered out of here.

When I finally reach the last leg, along School Road and around the bend, I see that most of Red House is already back, lining the embankment—even Emma has somehow beat me. I'm crying as I cross the finish line, and she rushes over to hug me. 'Well done,' she says.

'It's not well done,' I wail. 'It was . . . shit.'

But Emma laughs. 'You just finished the marathon, you dickhead. It's brilliant. Come on, let's cheer the others.'

So we sit there on the sweltering rocks, shouting down the slope. Many kids glance up the hill, startled at our hoarse cries—most of them I've never muttered a word to the whole year.

Then Kendall trundles around the corner, her long white hair tied back in a plait. She is breathing hard, forcing out the air, face strained like she's constipated. Emma and I get to our feet, cup our hands around our mouths and holler, 'Go, Kendall, you're almost home!'

A flicker moves across her contorted face. Her eyes stay focused, nailed to the finish line, and as she lurches forward, taking those final paces, she turns and raises a hand to us before falling to the ground.

~

I'm standing on the deck overlooking the road. Behind me Kendall rummages in her enormous case, the one Sarah pooed in. We're the last Red House girls up here. Everyone else has gone.

Lou was the first. She left before breakfast so she could make her flight to Canada where her family is skiing over Christmas. Emma left soon after, her mum waiting in the station wagon at the bottom of the hill. 'Will I see you again?' she sobbed, clinging to me. I keep forgetting she won't be at the Big School next year with the rest of us, that she's going back to Mildura forever. All this time I thought she would change her mind.

'Yeah, 'course,' I said, my own voice bloodless. I can't imagine what it's going to be like, not seeing her every day. 'And we'll talk on the phone heaps.'

She wiped her eyes, smiling. 'I forgot about phones,' she said.

On the other side of the dorm, Ronnie and Briohny and a couple of other girls had formed a circle around Portia. They were all talking loudly, drowning out the rest of the noise in the dorm, and I gave them a small, spiteful look as I crouched in front of my drawers to finish the last of my packing. All I could hear was laughter, and Portia's shrill insistence that they hang out over the holidays, at parties in the city and at the invite-only tennis tournament at a beach somewhere. Portia had invited me to the same event, even suggesting we partner up for doubles; I snorted at the memory of it. She glanced across the beds to me, raising a dark eyebrow. I gazed back at her, my face set, musing on how I couldn't, no matter how hard I tried, picture her on her own, without her girls, outside this dorm. She was shapeless, like a sea mist. And while I felt like she knew a lot about me—how to hurt me, how to lure me back—I really knew nothing about her at all.

I wonder now, standing on the deck, if she ever thought about her behaviour and how it made us all feel. What was it about Kendall that made Portia target her so relentlessly? And would she be like this next year, at the senior school? This thought sends a shiver down my spine.

I lean against the banister and peer over the unmoving campus. The others all left on the Melbourne buses. Most of the teachers have gone too—to their own families, or on holiday somewhere. I can't imagine Miss Lacey out there in the real world either, on a crowded city street, or lying on a beach. I wonder what Libby is doing for the holidays. I'd hoped to see her before I left, but that now seems unlikely.

Kendall joins me by the banister. Not too close, but it feels companionable. She rests her chin against her knuckles, sighing as she stares over the trees. 'Can't believe it's over,' she says.

I make a sound like a grunt. I feel shy out here with her.

'What have you got planned for the holidays?' she asks.

'Dunno,' I say. 'Go to the beach, maybe.'

She smiles. 'Sounds nice. I'll probably just catch up with some friends, then hang out at home, doing nothing.'

I look at her dumbly. I suppose she does have friends outside of school. Why wouldn't she? Kendall squints against the sun, still facing out over the school. And I realise that, like Portia, I never got to know Kendall—not any real part of her—even after living together for a whole year.

A silver sedan rolls up, gravel crunching beneath the wheels. 'That's my ride,' Kendall murmurs, a broader smile spreading across her face. She drags her suitcase across the deck and down the steps. The wheels make great thunks.

'Have a nice holiday, Bec,' she calls.

I raise a hand. 'Bye, Kends.'

She continues down the path, but stops under the banksia tree, turning back. 'You know,' she says, 'I think we're in the same day house next year. Boyd, right?'

'Yeah, that's right.'

Kendall nods. 'See you next year, then.'

She throws her suitcase in the boot of the sedan and climbs in. I can't see the driver, only their outline turned towards me. The car rolls on towards the utility track, taking the corner slowly, and disappears.

Now I'm alone. In the empty house, the floor is dusty, marked in places from the beds scraped across the polish. I walk the length of the aisle and I press my forehead against the window. It is cool, at first, but after a while it grows warm, my breath making a fog against the glass.

27

I wake early. My back is stiff, and my eyes are crusty from last night's crying. Groaning, I worm my way out of the sleeping bag. The rest of the campsite is still asleep. How quiet it is, like there is no one else in the world.

Throwing on my coat I wander towards the river and splash water on my face. The water is arctic, but it wakes me up. I wash my hands until they start to numb then take a few sips, gargling, and spit in the bushes.

Back at the tent I check my phone. I don't have any reception, so I scroll to an earlier message from Liv, wishing me luck on my way to Silver Creek.

As I have got older, friendship has become less complicated. These days I have a wonderful group of close friends: Liv, and Simone, who is now married and is a detective, and Anna, who is also my business partner—together we started a literary journal.

There are other friends, of course—new people coming into my life all the time—and each day I feel more open and more confident around them. I've finally lost that wariness.

My friends helped me get back on my feet after Alexis. They did the usual things we all do with friends at such a time, taking me shopping and out to dinner, and simply encouraging me to talk about how I was feeling, even when it tasted poisonous in my mouth. But I was so touched by the immediacy of their kindness; I had forgotten the depth of feeling you have with your friends—how much you love them. It was because of them that I began to let go of so much of what had happened in the past—Silver Creek, Kendall, Portia, Alexis—and to forgive myself.

Six months later I got my licence back and started driving to work again, with a breathalyser fitted to the car. I kept seeing Mary, because talking to her twice a week made me feel more in control of my emotions and helped me better understand my behaviour. And I began to teach myself that it is possible to have a healthy relationship with the past, especially when it is shared with others over such a long period of time.

While my head began to clear, there were still times when I felt that darkness scraping at me—I don't think that will ever go away. That tendency to be frightened of what other people think of me, coupled with that impulse drawing me to people who could do me harm. 'You can't change your impulses,' Mary once told me. 'But you can at least try to understand them.'

Once, during a session with Mary, I told her about a dream. I was back at Silver Creek, where a girl stood at the bottom of the vast driveway. Her back to me, she waited near the letterbox, slashing at the grass with a long stick. And there she stood, slashing and slashing, the noise growing louder and louder, until I had woken up to the weak light streaming through my bedroom blinds, drenched in sweat, my heart pounding.

'Even though I was just standing there, it was like I was being chased,' I'd said to Mary. 'That was the fear I woke up with: that someone was hunting me down.'

Recently I saw Portia in the city. I hadn't laid eyes on her since school, but I knew it was her even before she turned to face me—it was an electric current of knowing, something almost primal about it, because the hairs on the back of my neck actually bristled.

Immediately I turned away, and so did she, and then we'd stood at the traffic lights, only a few paces from each other. When the lights went green she lurched out onto the road, charging ahead with that familiar, arrogant swagger. I fell back, shrinking into the scarf wrapped high around my face, and when I looked up again she was gone.

That's what the girls are like: shadows. Ghosts. Always lurking at the edge of my memory, nudging like a boat tied loose to a jetty. I'm terrified of seeing them, of being confronted, chased, not only at Silver Creek but *anywhere*. Only now I am uncertain as to why. Is it because of what happened up in Red House, or is it because I have decided to bring them back to life?

I don't like to imagine them as adults. I think that's why I avoided Portia. For me, they will always be girls—baggy and imperfect. Kendall, especially. I know nothing about her life after school. What has become of her? Is she happy? These kinds of questions still plague me.

~

I pack up quickly. Campers are starting to emerge from tents, and a few fires are going. The sizzle of bacon in the pan wafting along in the air makes my stomach growl. Getting into the car, I wave to the couple at the next site, and further along the road a few boys kicking a football stop to watch me drive past.

Kendall and I did end up at senior school together, in the same house and in a few of the same classes. She still didn't seem to have many friends, but she did have some.

In our final year we shared an English class. Our rooms were on the other side of the campus, and we always walked to and from lessons together, chatting amicably—far more than we ever spoke at Silver Creek. We never mentioned Red House, or what happened up there. If she held a grudge, she never showed it. I've not met many people in my life with that kind of fortitude, that kind of courage.

Rolling over the bridge, I look down to the dark river. I'm searching for that branch trapped under the stones, but I can't see it. It must have come loose last night and washed away.

I drive on, along the rocky track, and when I come out of the trees, back onto the main road, I get reception again. There's a message waiting there, from Elinor: *Looking forward to tonight x.*

~

That night I arrive at the Kelvin early. Sitting at the corner table I tug at the hem of my dress. I'm nervous. I hadn't known what to wear for this date, but Liv had suggested, without hesitation, 'That dusky pink number of yours.'

Now I feel overdressed, overeager. If only I could have a drink to calm my nerves, and I stare longingly at the bottles of wine lining the shelf behind the counter.

My phone pings with a message. It's Elinor—she's running half an hour late. I glance at the wine again, feeling the faintest prickle of irritation. But then I find myself smiling, a smile so wide it hurts my face. It doesn't matter. This still feels like the start of something special.

ACKNOWLEDGEMENTS

During the early stages of crafting *Bad Behaviour* I was lucky enough to form a writing group, and as such I am indebted to Jo Case, Rochelle Siemienowicz, Serje Jones and Estelle Tang for their thoughtful responses and constant encouragement about the chapters in progress.

I'd also like to give special thanks to Kate Goldsworthy and Hannah Kent for reading early versions of the manuscript and for their insightful feedback that was crucial to shaping the book.

An enormous thank you to Jane Palfreyman, my wonderful publisher, for her unwavering enthusiasm and delicate guidance as the book developed into a living, breathing thing; to Ali Lavau for her brilliant copyediting; and to Belinda Lee and everyone at Allen & Unwin. Thanks, too, to Sandy Cull for the cover design.

To my agent, Pippa Masson, and all at Curtis Brown, thank you.

Many thanks to my colleagues at Text Publishing for their continued enthusiasm and support for my writing.

And last, but not least, to Elinor Griffith—thank you for your love and for always believing in me.

Rebecca Starford is publishing director of *Kill Your Darlings* magazine. Her debut novel, *The Imitator*, was published by Allen & Unwin in 2021. She lives in Brisbane with her partner and son.